TotallyReal

A blueprint to reboot your life

ELIZABETH CARNEY

Totally Real

First published in 2021 by

Panoma Press Ltd
48 St Vincent Drive, St Albans, Herts, AL1 5SJ, UK
info@panomapress.com
www.panomapress.com

Book layout by Neil Coe.

978-1-784529-32-1

The right of Elizabeth Carney to be identified as the author of this work has been asserted in accordance with sections 77 and 78 of the Copyright, Designs and Patents Act 1988.

A CIP catalogue record for this book is available from the British Library.

Dedication

I dedicate this book to my amazing son Patrick (Paddy) Kelly who has always been a joy and an inspiration; you kept me going when times were tough, always knowing how to be uniquely you, following your dreams, staying authentic and keeping it all Totally Real.

Sponsors

A big thank you to my sponsors:

VRS Precision Engineering Ltd

Serena Sinanan and Amber Cole

Paddy Carney

Diana Blakeman

Jo Thilwind - Dreamspace Art

Rosanna Monachello

Mitra Vijay - Mindful You

Praise for this book

"I was impressed… I found it extremely interesting, well written and really well thought out. It isn't so much a book to read but a discussion with the reader and the author."

Jilly Reffold, Retired Head Teacher

"Elizabeth speaks from her heart. It is clear to see how her experiences have influenced and impacted her perception of herself and the world. She has found the courage to speak up and in so doing has gained invaluable insight into who she is and what her purpose in life is all about. This informative, practical and humorous book is filled with integrity and a determination to help others find out who they truly are and live a happy and fulfilled life on their terms. Congratulations Elizabeth for finally giving this book your expertise and you to the world."

Brenda Dempsey, Publisher

"The best coach I have ever had… Elizabeth asks challenging questions and will not let me off the hook until I understand the deeper meaning. She has helped me to explore difficult places and emotions, revealing truths I have always avoided. This has significantly changed my thinking and the future direction of my life."

Kenneth Spencer, Driving School Owner

"This is your time to make a change. This year has allowed us to reflect on our past, shape our present and plan change in our future. It's time to take action and this book delivers a clear framework so you can create your own blueprint for success!"

Nicky Chisholm, Director, Mumpreneurs Networking Club (MNC)

"A great and useful read covering so many areas in an easy to apply manner. From identity to influence, and even how we can at times be sabotaging the very relationships that we need the most. It helps us to stand out in a way that is congruent with who we really are, and I love the ten-step reality check! READ IT!"

David Hyner, Researcher and Speaker

Acknowledgements

Patrick – My world – Mr Sunshine from the moment you were born, you shine your light on the dark places of us all.

Mum – For always believing in me, even when I didn't believe in myself and never giving up even when the words didn't come out quite right or weren't received as intended.

My Brother and Sisters – guaranteed to always keep it *'Totally Real'*. Pass the cornflakes!

To Dad, and family and friends who are no longer with us – you have walked with me at times in my life and all played a part in getting me to where I am now.

Lenise Shaw – You found me when I was hobbling around on crutches; a chance meeting that set me on a path of exploration where I discovered and trained in a range of different healing modalities that are now inextricably woven into my life and my work.

All my colourful ladies – Rebecca White, Diana Blakeman, Jane Cooke, Lesley Wrankmore. You showed me that colour is the new black and helped me to come out from the shadows to show the world the real vibrant me in my true colours.

My nieces, nephews, aunts, uncles, cousins, the wider extended family, friends, colleagues and the rest, because without you I would not be me.

Anne Jones for the Foreword, the love, the light, clearing, healing, friendship and support.

Angie Phillips of A.N.G. Design Consultancy for the cover logo.

Mindy and all the team at Panoma Press who have made this dream a reality.

Contents

Foreword

Everyone at some time in their life will face the trauma of loss, whether it be self-confidence, self-worth, motivation or direction. Most of us have had times of complete despair: a marriage fails, a loved one leaves, a career stalls. You may have also realised that somewhere along the way from childhood to where you are today, you have even lost yourself!

It takes bravery, honesty and help to get through all of the above but the hardest truth to admit and heal is that you are not the person you thought you were. To accept that you may have spent years putting on a mask, pretending to enjoy, pretending to approve and accepting bad behaviour from those close to you. To know that you have focused on pleasing those close to you, either at work or home, rather than the needs of your own heart and soul, the needs of the hidden real you.

Elizabeth has written the most inspiring and motivating book for anyone whose life has crashed or who wishes to find their true self. She has evolved a way to recalibrate and regenerate our lives when all feels lost. She shows us how to discover who we really are and what we really want from our life. She guides us gently to rebuild what has failed and to pick ourselves up and start again to find our way forward.

Throughout her book Elizabeth raises questions that I recommend you take time to answer. She will probe you to look within and see whether you are accepting and living consciously with your true self. She gives you permission to sit back and evaluate your life and guides you to release fears and suppressed emotions and reveal hidden passions and lost dreams. She shares ways to move forward to accepting and believing that whatever your dreams, whatever your feelings, you are perfectly OK.

I spend my working life as a spiritual teacher and healer persuading my clients to accept their uniqueness, to understand that their genetics and life experiences have made them different from everyone else in this world and that makes them special, not a failure, not someone to be ashamed of. I help them heal their negative beliefs about themselves and to move on from trauma. Healing is accepting and caring for oneself, finding the love and value within oneself, despite the traumas of life.

Elizabeth has written an essential book for that journey of healing and acceptance. She will help you whether you are in a confidence crisis, lost and confused about life, or have a need to heal your perception of yourself. She will guide you to discover the divide between the real you and the pretend you and for discovering your uniqueness.

This book is clever and inspiring and will help you to recalibrate your view of yourself, to guide you away from seeing yourself as the role you play, to help you to drop the masks, to let go the pretence and to discover the real you, then you can make the life choices that serve you best.

Anne Jones

Author and Healer

"We shall not cease from exploration
And the end of all our exploring
Will be to arrive where we started
And know the place for the first time."

T S Eliot

Preface

My mission is to wake people up to their unique brand of awesomeness. Through the journey of this book you will discover how one person's disappearance into invisibility and return to totally real evolved into a blueprint to reboot your life. At every stage there are thought-provoking questions and activities to guide you on an exploration of your own. I uncover key patterns to be aware of, and introduce the Reboot Protocol, guiding you through the steps to reconnect with your true self to create a life you love, and live on your terms.

When you have finished reading (or perhaps before), your new journey will begin, because you will have stepped out from the shadows and into the light. You will remember what you have forgotten, recognise all that has been suppressed and you will be aware of your beautiful soul. You will know that you are unique. You will reconnect with your inner self and understand what it means to be you. You will rediscover the wisdom that you were born with, as the path you have taken up to now is revealed with all its twists and turns, detours, roadblocks and dead ends. You will be clear on where this path has taken you and how you managed to stay on it for so long.

The road ahead will become clear and you will discover the vehicle to enable you to travel unimpeded in the direction you are meant to go. People will come and go; some may leave your journey – perhaps of their own accord or some because you ask them to; others will join you as new travelling companions. Your new companions will be heading in the same direction as you, and most importantly they will lift you up and help you to stay on track. They will not bring you down or attempt to bend you to their will or control you for their own purposes. You will be free. You will be visible. You will have found your own voice; you will be strong enough to stand (and stay) in your own power. You will know that you are enough and recognise your rights as an individual. You will be proud to say I am ME!

This book will not give you **all** the answers, because your journey is yours and yours alone. Everything you do is of your choosing – whatever happens is a direct result of those choices. What you will find, however, is a guide, a map if you like that illuminates your journey so far, so that you can see it clearly: the hills you climbed that you could have gone round, the deserts where you wandered seeking water to quench your thirst, the forests where you were lost and desperately seeking a way out, the motorway that took you round in circles unable to find the correct exit. This book will help you to see where you have been and how you came to be in those places.

The knowledge that comes from that understanding will show you that there is another way and you will be able to see the right exit, the path through the forest, the oasis in the desert and the clear route round the hills. It won't tell you which way to go but it will show you that there are options. You will become aware that those options are available to you and it is within your own power to select the next stage of your journey, knowing that this is the real, authentic road that you are meant to travel.

How you get to the start of that journey will involve making some changes. You will need to be clear on why you are making the journey; what is your purpose? Your objective? Who is going with you and who is not? How are you travelling? Where are you going? Above all, what are you leaving behind? What no longer serves you? This stage may still be a bit rocky and full of obstacles – let's not forget that this is the familiar and you are stepping into something new. Inevitably there will be a pull back because this is all you know up to now. Once you commit, however, there is no going back, because when you have seen what you need to, there is no way to un-see.

The start of every journey as they say begins with a single step, so if any of this resonates with you then please invest in yourself, read this book so you too can journey back home, reboot your life and be fully visible as your authentic self!

"Beauty begins the moment you
decide to be yourself."

Coco Chanel

Prologue

The old woman looked in the mirror and sighed for the memory of what she had once been: sparkling eyes, beautiful skin, a smile that lit up a room. A smile that intrigued, caressed and reached her eyes, a smile full of promise and hope. A shadow stared back at her – a dull, lifeless, grey shadow. Faded eyes dimmed by life and despair reflected back a haunted look that told the story of broken dreams and betrayal – and tears, too many tears. An ocean of tears that left her almost numb – almost but not quite.

The old woman stared at the ghostly image looking back at her, the face that measured out her life; the hurts grooved out in every wrinkle that marched across pale skin – stark, deep and meticulously formed, as the pain that caused them. She remembered J Alfred Prufrock who 'measured out his life with coffee spoons' and 'the women that come and go talking of Michelangelo'. Lines fixed in memory and time from school days long gone. Pointless, meaningless words, or are they? Why after so many years do they continue to keep her company? Still with her, reminding her of the futility and inevitability of everything.

She studies that ancient visage with quiet reflection yet anger coils, wormed deep into every cell of her being. Rage at the injustices, the broken promises, the lies, the cover-ups, the breaking of spirit, the cold silence, and at the forefront, above all of it, the white-hot rage of her acquiescence in all of this. How had she allowed it to happen? Where was that carefree child that dreamed of riding bareback, joining the circus, llama trekking in Peru, swimming in the blue lagoon and living happily ever after in a wondrous castle with her handsome prince?

Where was the idealistic young woman who was going to forge her own memorable path, do great things and write about them, the girl who would change lives and change the world? Where was she? Where had she gone? How had she allowed the life to be sucked out of her? Why had she given in to the demands of other people, gone along with what they wanted, not spoken up for herself? When had she started simply to fit in? When did she lose her voice? When had she become invisible?

And yet, she wasn't entirely invisible, was she? Shadowy – yes, quiet – yes, broken – perhaps? Perhaps!

Looking old and tired and grey and wrinkled – did I say tired? Yes, so tired, so little energy, no fight left in her. She was washed up. She had had enough and she didn't know where to go or what to do next. There really was no one to turn to – no one understood. She had tried to explain and they were clueless, just thought she was crazy or had drunk too much wine. There were people around her – family, friends, she was almost never entirely on her own but she had never felt so lonely or alone. Well-meaning attempts to help simply added to the pain, enhanced the feelings of being different, created inarticulate inability to explain and rebounded with additional anger, frustration and despair.

She looked in the mirror and asked herself why? Once again she cried, a bitter irony in these tears that freely flowed. Once upon a time she never cried. She was an expert at bottling up – everything safely stored away inside. Then one day someone came along – her handsome prince perhaps. He taught her how to cry, then made her cry and now was long gone – scar-like wrinkled grooves the only outward sign of his passing through her life.

So, she continued to look at this old face in the mirror and at first she was sad at what she saw, at what she had become. Then suddenly something made her look a little harder, deeper maybe. She gritted her teeth, clenched her fists and tensed every muscle in her body. Something made her look past what she could see on the surface. A flicker of something buried deep forced her to look through the mirror, beyond the glass and through to her core. Through the sorrow of her tears anger rose, a spark flashed in her eyes, and as her fingernails carved deep crescents into both of her hands she forced this 'thing' to the surface and with grim determination faced it for the first time. She stared that sad reflection down and she spoke aloud: "Enough, no more, I will never be invisible again."

The old woman was not really old. The year was 2011, she was 51. She was ME!

For many, this may have heralded the starting point of the happy ever after, but for me at this time it was simply another start-over – another new beginning. It was, however, a new phase of learning and growth. It began with the realisation that I had spent over 25 years of my life trying to fit in. I had made every effort to fit into a corporate world that in return remorselessly crushed my spirit, robbed me of my voice, questioned my integrity and subjected me to bullying by persons of limited intellectual capacity who had been promoted way beyond their capabilities.

Ultimately, I questioned my every thought and action and worried myself stupid in the process. I made every attempt to fit in. I endeavoured to do all that was asked, working crazy hours to achieve incredible results for no thanks or acknowledgement. I even had to suffer the indignity of my successes being claimed as the work of others. I learned that it was pointless to challenge 'them'. The more I attempted to fit in, to comply with what they said they wanted, to dress the right way, to speak the right speak, learn all the jargon, pass the exams – the more I did all of this, the more invisible I became. Exceeding every target they ever gave me was not good enough, neither was saving millions of pounds. Finally, one day 'they' decided to dispense with my services altogether.

Don't get me wrong, I didn't hate all of my years with the big corporates – only the last few where the management style of choice left much to be desired and demonstrated by the most senior in a manner totally at odds with the training given to new managers. Go Figure! – as my American friends would exclaim in such incongruous situations. I had an extraordinary career with the privilege of working across the globe, meeting many amazing people and learning fantastic skills along the way. As a result, I have a huge number of qualifications and incredible experience that I defy anyone to emulate! I don't say this to brag about my achievements, rather to give thanks to fate and circumstances that put me in the way of being able to participate in this adventure of a life that has been fully lived in all its ups and downs.

The end of 2011 dumped me unceremoniously into one of the lowest points in my life. I was physically, mentally and emotionally drained. I was alone and with no job and no clue what to do next. There was no husband or partner to listen, help or support. There was no financial or any other buffer, just a huge void into which I had fallen, a black hole that had sucked up my confidence. I felt helpless in a hopeless situation and I had no clue anymore who I was. It was as if my relationships with people and companies had marooned me on an alien planet with no familiar reference points, nothing to steer or guide me and I was clearly lost. At this stage, a map or a compass or even the stars would have been of little use – I no longer knew *what* to do with them but more importantly I had no idea *where* I wanted to go. I didn't't know *why* I wanted to go anywhere and certainly had no clue *how* I was going to do anything about the state I was in.

A good friend of mine often says, "It is not what happens to you but the way you deal with what happens that makes the difference to what you achieve." In 2011 I had not met this individual or heard this statement but looking back I can now see the absolute truth in this and the sentiment resonates on a daily basis. Everyone has stuff to deal with and the way you deal with your particular stuff is what delivers the results you ultimately get. Sitting around moaning, blaming everyone else, and yes crying about it will not achieve much but simply more of the same. Plastering on a smile, taking action and asking what can I learn from this situation is a great place to start changing things.

The invisible, voiceless shadow that I had become by 2011 managed to dig deep, to find a spark, hold on to a ray of hope and climb back out of that dark place and into the light. I would love to say it has been an easy journey but that is not the case and there have been false starts, blind alleys, red herrings, ever decreasing circles and all manner of other obstacles thrown at me in the years since I looked at the old woman in the mirror. I am proud of being able to say that I didn't give up and I will never give up. The last few years have been another incredible journey with all the ups and downs of such a journey; friends have come and gone, thankfully some have stayed the course, others have come back into my life and still more have simply arrived and connected and our journey together has begun.

I am a firm believer in the saying that 'People come into your life for a reason, a season or a lifetime'. Sometimes it is hard to work out which until they are gone, and of course it is not always easy to let them go – more on that later. This is not just about friends though, there is much more to the story. This book is the culmination of that story and more. It is the end of one phase and the beginning of another. The amazing thing to me, and I hope for you later, is that if you are reading this – I got here. I have come out from the dark place where the invisible woman lived and through my winding journey have picked up my colour, my life, my vitality, my joy. I have found my voice and I speak to you now with confidence and also with love because I am back – once again I am ME!

My wish for you is that you never lose your sense of self, your identity, the uniqueness that is the essence of you and that you never ever feel invisible or without voice and that you are always in touch with your 'mojo' – your own individual 'me'. If you feel that you have lost all or part of your mojo, my sincere wish is that as you read through this book and follow my journey you will discover things that will resonate and signposts to help you to find your way back. If you have never experienced this kind of loss, I give you my blueprint to ensure that you never do.

"The coolest people I've ever met have the most colourful pasts, they've lived lives of risk, made bad choices, learned lessons, explored, and they're not afraid of being real. Tattered tapestries woven of similar threads, they're my kind of people.

My favourite shades of crazy."

Stephen L Lisotte

Chapter 1

Totally me – journey to fully visible

How it all began

Before I get into the detail of the rest of the journey from 2011 to now (2020) or more importantly the essence of my blueprint for getting your 'me' back or never losing it in the first place, it's only fair to give you a little more information on who I am and essentially the story of my beginnings, what I started with, how I allowed myself to lose sight of me and to show how easy it is to let this happen without even being aware of what is going on.

I was born in Moseley, Birmingham almost 12 months after my parents were married. It was 1st August 1960 – my mother's 24th birthday. Dad always said that it made him a great husband – planning his wife's birthday present nine months in advance! Never was too sure if that's how Mum really wanted to celebrate her birthday and of course we have been sharing our birthday ever since. All I will say is sharing a birthday with your mother is not always the easiest thing to deal with. Naturally some have been more memorable than others for all the right and wrong reasons. Suffice to say milestones have always been celebrated and plenty of cake and bubbles have been consumed including one year when we had four cakes between us because typical family communication meant that everyone thought no one else had organised one!

I have a brother and two sisters who arrived at roughly three-year intervals in 1963, 1966 and 1969. Family life was increasingly noisy and of course there were plenty of cousins living locally too. Christmas and visits from the American side of the family were always a good excuse for family gatherings where Grandad would sing Irish folk songs and regale us with his tales of Tom Cat and the Big Brown Bear. The adventures of this unlikely pair were legendary in the family – Grandad's stories invariably involved a supporting cast of cockroaches and other gruesome creatures appearing from underneath the garden shed or the rhubarb patch. There was always lots of running around and mayhem with either Tom Cat or the Big Brown Bear (he never did get a name) getting stuck up a tree or being chased off down the road – they always lived to appear in another tale.

My maternal grandparents provided a peaceful haven for sleepovers and to this day I can hear the ticking of the bedroom clock that lulled me to sleep on my special camp bed in their room. I still have the chest of drawers that was part of Granny's bedroom furniture and I swear to this day the fresh laundered smell of the linens she kept in the bottom drawer wafts out whenever I open it. Granny was an accomplished tailoress and my dolls and I were always immaculately kitted out with beautiful dresses that she appeared to run up in minutes.

A young Elizabeth aged about four years

Mum taught at a school in Henley-in-Arden and from when I was about three she used to take me to school with her – it was different in those days. I used to sit in the reception class and of course learned to read and write well before I was deemed old enough to go to school! My lifelong love of reading began when after about two weeks at proper school I had finished the entire official reading scheme and was given free rein to select whatever I wanted from the junior library.

I would literally lose myself in books, I was transported into the thick of the action: I was at Smugglers Top with The Famous Five, got shipwrecked with The Adventurous Four, went walkabout in Australia and had kaffee and kuchen with the chalet school girls in Switzerland. I would tuck myself into any quiet space I could find and be transported to far-off lands and crazy adventures. So was born the desire to travel that has never left me – there's plenty more still to do before I hang up the hiking boots and turn my skis into a cute wall decoration.

As expected, I passed the eleven-plus and was accepted to a top grammar school where I languished for the next five years. Sadly, for me anyway it didn't live up to all the hype and I was horribly disappointed. None of the teachers stood out as particularly inspiring and some of them were rather nasty to everyone. Looking back, I do wonder why on earth some of them were there. The teaching was archaic even then and I was horribly bored most of the time. There are very few outstanding memories and none that merit a mention here.

By the time we got to sixth form the borough had merged everyone into one sixth form college in a brand-new purpose-built campus. I think my year was only the second intake so it was all pretty fresh and exciting. We had lecturers not teachers and no school uniform and obviously it was co-ed – another adventure for us grammar school 'gels'. The main things I remember are that it was an even longer walk from the bus stops in the centre of town – not much fun in winter; there was also an amazingly eccentric Greek Orthodox teacher of philosophy who had a first degree in pure science and ran rings around us in any debate because he could argue the point most convincingly from any perspective we attempted to challenge.

To this fine gentleman with his ridiculously unfashionable Fair Isle sweaters, bicycle clips and blu-tacked spectacles I owe at least some recognition for advancing my cognitive development and showing the way to understanding and appreciating the merits of different perspectives. At the time much of what he introduced us to seemed to go straight over my head; with hindsight I now understand I learned more than I thought, I simply wasn't ready to process or use it. Just shows that we do actually absorb information even when we don't realise we are doing so. It's a shame that it has taken nearly 40 years for me to consciously recognise some of that teaching and be able to incorporate it in what I do.

Giving up on dreams

At 17 I wanted to be a cordon bleu chef and I had an amazing (for 1977) business idea that would follow on from this, but there were no places on the course I wanted to take for over two years. It seemed like an eternity, I couldn't wait that long and only one particular school would do. How easily I was deterred. I still love to cook, but it is with an ironic sense of hindsight that I see how others with those same dreams were not diverted and blazed a trail to become household names. My only regret, that I gave up too easily based on the opinions of those who believed that 'cooking' for a living was neither a professional nor lucrative career. Raymond Blanc, Jamie Oliver, Rick Stein, Gordon Ramsay and many more might have something to say about that.

At 18 I decided that I had done enough studying for a while, and as I couldn't do what I wanted, I got a job in a bank and promptly began studying for my banking exams. In 1978 this choice placed me squarely in a 'man's world' with a very solid glass ceiling. In addition, I really didn't take too well to the repetitiveness of much of the work and the stifling, spirit-crushing hierarchy, where opinions, creativity and change were not remotely encouraged. What on earth was I thinking?

I decided this was not for me and headed off to Wales where I acquired a degree in Communications Studies graduating with the belief that I would saunter immediately into an exciting media career of some sort. Needless to say, despite charming my way past various watchdogs into a short-term unpaid job at Central Television's sports department and hobnobbing with some seriously famous sports personalities of the day, it didn't happen.

I did get some paid freelance interviewing work for a local radio station but this was local radio not local to where I was. Consequently, any job I got required borrowing my grandad's car and driving great distances there and back and this just about used up the paltry fee I received to pay for the petrol to drive there and do the job in the first place. Did I love it? Yes. Was it exciting? Yes. But, and it was a huge BUT – everyone who thought they had a say in my life was constantly on at me to get a 'proper' job. There wasn't enough work, it wasn't sustainable, there was too much competition, why couldn't I just... and on and on it went until eventually of course I caved in. I listened and, once more, I gave up my dreams even as the faint glimmer of success was starting to reveal itself.

Stuck in the hamster wheel

Most of the next 25 years or so were spent on one corporate treadmill or another. Don't get me wrong – I had some great jobs, travelled a lot, worked with some amazing cultures and people. I was privileged to receive excellent training and I defy anyone to match my bizarre range of certificates and qualifications! I used to worry that I didn't have just a single professional qualification that entitled me to practise as a lawyer or an accountant for example, but now I realise that the breadth of my experience is unique and it is exactly why I am now able to do what I do. It is why I am able to write this book. It is also a huge factor in how I lost myself – my voice, my energy, my confidence and my self-belief – it is how I became invisible. Not literally of course but my sense of who I was had gone – everything that made me – well ME – was squashed and hidden from view. It was so hidden I couldn't even find 'me' myself.

So how did a highly educated, skilled and experienced senior manager and leader simply disappear like this? Obviously, it didn't happen overnight; it is a long slow gradual process that simply grinds relentlessly away at you as you go about achieving your allocated corporate tasks in the name of performance, targets and strategy. There is in some ways little difference between the daily treadmill of corporate life today and the slave-driving factories spawned by the industrial revolution. Conditions may be nicer in an office environment (if a sick building can be considered nicer than a dust-polluted cotton mill); however, the bullies have simply changed their clothes. Profit is still king and the dehumanisation and suppression of the workforce is as rife today as it ever was. This may sound like an extreme and jaded view of life in the corporate world and of course not all of it was bad, or at least not all of the time, but it has actually taken me years to understand how it worked and what it had actually done to ME!

Rather than dwell on the matter, I know now that the choices were mine. At the end of the day, I allowed it to happen. Anyone else involved was also caught up in the same unhappy trap – the trap that we walk willingly into, like mice after cheese. Like mice want cheese – we aim to please. We are trained from our school days to get the grades, to get a degree (the best qualifications we can), in order to get a good job, going to work to fill someone else's pockets. Someone who most likely neither knows us or even cares who we are as long as we just do what we are told.

The path to getting lost

Maybe, the naturally curious child is constantly told to shut up and be quiet when they are asking the natural, endless questions that will help them make sense of the world. The boundary-pushing teenager is historically forbidden to do all manner of activities because 'parents know best'. The eager student is bored to tears by hopeless lecturers who aim merely to get through the day rather than stimulate enquiring minds. The adult catapulted into the workplace is then repeatedly told not to ask questions but just do as they are told; asking questions gets one labelled as a troublemaker.

From the day we can talk, our basic instinct that helps us to make sense of the world and who we are is constantly suppressed. Some people give in sooner than others. Some fight for as long as they can until eventually the fight goes out of them. Essentially, the system wants us docile, wants us working, not for ourselves but somewhere we can be controlled until they decide they are done with us and we are retired into poverty. The dream they sold us about qualifications and fine jobs and fat salaries evaporates after years of servitude. The new reality is attempting to live on far less than we could live on when we were working. Retirement comes later and later – pensions have been mismanaged....

By the time we find out it is too late and we accept our fate, realising that we have now worked 'Forty hours a week for forty years to live on forty per cent of what we couldn't live on in the first place'.

Know your own value

A simple message here – if you don't love what you are doing, then don't do it. Find something you do love and do that. It won't feel like work and you will be much happier and in control of your own destiny. I hope you will anyway – more on that later. Love what you do. Do what you love. You are also totally in control of the hours you put in and the money you can earn – you can create and set your own *value*. Hold on to that thought because knowing your own value – understanding what you are worth – is a critical part of everything that I am going to be sharing with you in this book.

Love me do

Ah – I have gone and mentioned the love word so there is no skirting around the topic now. Let's face it, there is so much bad done in the name of love (and religion but that's another subject) that sometimes I wonder why we crave it so much. Perhaps the love we crave is not love at all but something else entirely. The love of a spouse, partner, significant other that starts with passion and excitement often turns into something far different from what was originally promised. The intricacies of our human journeys and the entanglement with others is not always the divine timing of a blissful existence that endures until 'death do us part'.

The end of a relationship, especially if unwanted, unplanned and unexpected at least by one of the people involved, can result in huge trauma that takes years to recover from. The fallout, in every sense of the word, may be huge. The emotions (shame, anger, guilt for example), the questioning of whether anything was ever real, if they ever really loved you, what on earth happened? And that is probably just the beginning, after which much more starts to unravel.

When you begin to question your role in the relationship, even where there was no domestic violence, were you actually allowing yourself to be controlled in the interests of the other person? How much of yourself had you given away to keep the peace, to keep the relationship on track? How often did you fail to listen to your intuition, or trust yourself and your own opinions? The more people I speak with, especially women unfortunately, the more I hear things like: "You're telling my story," "That's exactly what happened to me," "I don't know why I couldn't see it at the time." Sad but true. In some respects, everything and nothing has changed over the centuries.

A little investigation reveals some worrying statistics:

- Divorces are on the rise among the UK's over-50s. According to figures from the UK Office for National Statistics, the over-50s divorce rate increased by 5.8% in 2016 as compared to 2015. This is the first increase since 2009/10 and equates to 8.9 in every 1,000 married couples over the age of 50. In total, some 13,000 women aged 55 and over got divorced in 2016.

- *The Telegraph* – August 2020: 1 in 4 over-50s have been furloughed – 377,000 may never work again. Over-50s represent 32% of the UK workforce.

- Age UK highlight that ageism is still a key concern in the workplace with one in three 55- to 64-year-olds believing they have been disadvantaged because of their age.

- An article published by Considerable.com in June 2019 highlights that in 1990, for every 1,000 married Americans aged 50 or older, there were just five who got divorced. By 2015 the divorce rate for this group had doubled. They go on to say: 'After older adults have perhaps cared for dependent children, parents or other relatives, spouses may reassess their marriages and ask, "What's next?" "Who are you?" or, better yet, "Who am I?"' One of the people they interviewed, Laura, a 59-year-old woman who was married for 18 years, said this: "I was unhappy in year one and I stayed 17 more. I hoped that it would change. I didn't really have the courage to get out. I think a lot of people stay in… for fear of the unknown. It sort of takes your soul away."

- The redundancy rate for those in their 50s is more than double the rate for those in their 40s according to research from over-50s jobs site Rest Less (Agediscrimination.info – 1 November 2019); for the period April to June 2019, 31,000 people in their 50s were made redundant.

- As a result of being made redundant from a senior executive role at 50, Tamar Posner became a psychotherapist, so she has had personal experience of the transitions that people in middle age sometimes need to make. "Part of it is existential. Most of us have had death anxiety as children, but it resurfaces when we are less distant from death."

She found that many of her clients were feeling lonely and isolated. "Thoughts would go round and round in their heads with no capacity to do anything other than get bigger! Usually these were people whose lives had been busy and productive but that had ended, through retirement or redundancy.

"Or their work had been looking after the home and family, but the children had left, or they'd been widowed or separated. There was no one to talk to. Their experience resonated with what I'd been through, ten years earlier, and I thought how much easier it would have been if I hadn't been isolated." https://high50.com/life/therapy-for-over-50s-how-it-feels-to-be-50

- According to a 2017 NBC article by Larry Alton: "There's a belief that low self-esteem goes hand in hand with incompetence and apathy... and 85 per cent of people suffer from low self-esteem."

The conclusion I draw from the above findings is simply – it's not just me then! Hopefully you will also realise that it is not just you either. You are not alone, and it is also important to reinforce that it is not your fault either. Sure, we make choices, but much of our 'programming' is set in place far earlier in life. This creates the default patterns for how we then react to what happens in our lives.

I have already alluded to the nature of parental love that (and not always with the wrong intention) clips our wings instead of teaching us to fly. I see overprotective parents do everything for their children, so they do not learn how to think for themselves or develop any independence. I also see parents who are so busy with the jobs that they work at to provide for their family that they do not have time to play with their kids, to answer their questions, read to them, show them how to build relationships. I see parents who tell their children they can be anything they want to be, do anything they want, and at the first sign of any expression of independence give a thousand reasons why something cannot be done, so they lose their belief.

No, not now, shut up, be quiet, maybe, later… Still as relevant now as ever. Research highlights the following shocking findings:

- **The average two-year-old child hears 432 negative statements per day,** but only 32 positive statements each day, according to a research study at the University of Iowa.

- **Children with unhealthy self-esteem feel that the important adults and peers in their lives do not accept them,** do not care about them very much, and would not go out of their way to ensure the child's safety and wellbeing, according to Prof Lissette Saavedra's article in *Psychology of Infancy & Childhood*.

Is it any wonder so many arrive in adulthood with a negative default pattern?

I remember reading at school and actually being rather shocked at the time by this poem from Philip Larkin:

> "They fuck you up, your mum and dad.
> They may not mean to, but they do.
> They fill you with the faults they had
> And add some extra, just for you.
>
> But they were fucked up in their turn
> By fools in old-style hats and coats,
> Who half the time were soppy-stern
> And half at one another's throats.
>
> Man hands on misery to man.
> It deepens like a coastal shelf.
> Get out as early as you can,
> And don't have any kids yourself."

It does rather sum up exactly what I am attempting to explain and serves to highlight exactly how and where our 'Me-ness' can be stealthily eroded over the years until we no longer know or even care about the things that were once of vital importance to us. It may well be that for some folk that is perfectly fine, they go through life and accept their lot and have no desire for anything to be different. I guess that as you are reading this book something in you has triggered a need to change.

You may be asking questions such as:

- Is this all there is?

- Where has my life gone?

- Why am I so unhappy?

- Why am I frightened?

- Why does no one listen to what I say?

- Why can't I find love?

- Who am I anyway?

You may be thinking things like:

- I hate my job

- I am bored

- I can't seem to get ahead

- My life is unexciting

- I have nothing to look forward to

- Nobody cares about me

- I don't care about me

The whole point of this book is to show you how it doesn't have to be this way, how knowing the signs and how to deal with them can stop you heading down this road. If you are reading this and thinking I am already too far down this road, don't worry. It's never too late and you can find your way back if you want to. That's the key – you do have to put in some effort though.

The first step is to *acknowledge* your current situation, then you must want to change it, you need to truly *believe* you can change things and then discover *exactly* what you need to change before you *plan* and then take *action* to make the changes. Finally, you need to add a safety net to catch you when you fall. It is not likely to be easy and you will more than likely slip back into some of your old ways before you have fully embedded the changes you have made. As long as you are able to recognise what is happening and have a strategy for putting it right again then it will be OK. Trust me – **it will be OK!**

We are human after all and it's in our nature to slip up, to backslide, to have a cheat day when we are dieting for example. So, let's consider the changes we are talking about (even if you don't know what they are yet!) in the context of weight loss. What happens when we decide it's time to lose weight?

1. We acknowledge the current situation We see that we are bigger, heavier, flabbier and unhealthier than we would like to be.

2. We decide that we want to change this situation – truly we do – yes really, we do. How many times have we really, really wanted to lose weight, get healthier or fitter?

3. Before we begin we truly believe that we can do it. We can change.

4. We investigate exactly what approach we are going to take and make a plan to start on Monday (it's always Monday isn't it?). On Monday we join the gym, start eating clean, drink our shakes, go somewhere for somebody else to tell us how much we weigh, take up running, eat cabbage; there are hundreds of ways and it's different strokes for different folks.

5. It is Monday and we are off. Everything always goes well to start with. We are fired up and excited and after a while we start seeing a difference – on the scales, with our energy levels, maybe our skin is clearer, our clothes start to get loose and all is well. Then **BOOM!** Life happens. At this point where we got annoyed or upset about something, we may give into temptation, eat cake, drink alcohol, do any of things we had sworn off. So what? As long as we get back on the plan then we will be fine.

6. The safety net – knowing, understanding and sharing our goals, being accountable, having a support group, forgiving ourselves, being determined, repeat steps one to five until the life events no longer derail us.

What I am talking about in the context of rebooting your life, becoming fully visible, living life on your terms and ultimately transforming your soul is the same process – well the steps are the same, the content is different that's all. In order to make the changes we want, we have to know where we are now and exactly what the problem is, so that we can understand the root causes before we can create a vision for the future and create sustainable transformational change.

"You did not come here to be normal,
you came here to be you."

Robert Holden

Chapter 2

Shit happens and then you live!

Yes – shit happens and then you LIVE! You are probably wondering if you read that right, because the familiar recognisable saying is of course 'Shit happens and then you die.' Phrases like this one and 'Life's a bitch' popularised in the 1980s are now part of our everyday language, so much so that they have moved from urban myth to the realm of self-fulfilling prophecy. We hear these phrases so often and I'll take a bet that when bad things happen to us these are the sorts of things we say to ourselves – and to others around us for that matter.

So, guess what? The universe hears us and provides exactly what we ask for – more negativity and more of what we don't really want, because that's exactly what we are focused on. However, I digress, because what I actually want to talk about is precisely the opposite. It doesn't have to be that way. It's possible to create a shift and make a positive change to get your life where you want it to be.

If you are reading this, I expect that on some level you are not currently where you want to be. I imagine like many of us you have been living your life and mostly everything has been OK. Of course, there have been ups and downs – that's what life is all about after all, but on balance you've probably been motoring through the years, ticking off your life boxes. You like and maybe even love your work, your job. You think you have a good marriage and a happy family life. You may not be rich, but life is comfortable. You are comfortable – everything is as it should be in your world. Then one day – BOOM! It's not OK. You are not OK, and you wonder if anything will ever be OK again.

Whatever happened to change your world virtually overnight has shocked you to your core. You don't know who you are any more and you don't know what to do. The strong capable person you have always believed yourself to be has vanished in the blink of an eye. Your head is now all over the place, you are possibly drinking far too much and eating far too little.

To the outside world, however, you put on a good show and everyone thinks you are coping amazingly well, because that's what you want them to think. Inside though, it's a different story altogether: inside you are suffocating, struggling to breathe, crying, screaming, swearing, crying some more. You are lost, lonely and question everything about who you are. The person you thought you were has suddenly become invisible and your identity has disappeared. Your challenge now is to find it again, to move beyond the shit, to live life again and to live it your way.

Invisibility – hiding in plain sight

The biggest problem I found is that as a strong capable woman I didn't realise what had actually happened to me until a long time after those significant life changes. I mean, I didn't understand the emotional toll events had taken on me; I couldn't see how it wasn't only the significant happenings – the betrayal, the divorce, the redundancy – that brought me finally to the turning point where everything suddenly became clear. Much happens in the course of a lifetime but often it takes something huge for us to see exactly how we too have responsibility for where we find ourselves, when we wake up to the need for change.

Working through my own journey and also with many accomplished women who have hit that brick wall or had that door slammed in their face and ended up wondering what they did to deserve it, I have discovered an all too familiar pattern. That pattern shows up as one of making our true selves invisible; we wear the masks of our chosen identities until one day we no longer have those identities and the masks are no longer required. The problem is how do we step out from that hiding place? How do we find out who we really are?

I have identified a number of common ways that people knowingly or unknowingly make themselves invisible. The scale of invisibility can be perceived on a spectrum, as can all of the individual contributing factors. Almost everyone I speak with on this subject has said that to some degree they currently feel or have at some stage in their life felt invisible. They believe they don't have a voice any more, or personal power, and often no longer really know who they are. They are, however, able to recognise themselves and the outcomes of their behaviours in each of the areas I have identified.

To be honest, everyone has a different journey and some people tell me that they have been there and come out the other side. To others it is like turning the light on and they can finally see what is going on. For some, all aspects are relevant and others only a few. It is also possible to be at different stages of the spectrum for any combination of the factors involved. From here, however, it is possible to make a start on the inner work required to get out of an unwanted situation and to work towards becoming the best possible version of you, Totally Real, and *fully visible* in any way you want to be.

I knew I had to explore this further to ensure other people didn't have to go through this debilitating experience on their own. By drawing on my extensive network and research experience, I immersed myself in the fallout of a sudden lack of status. It threw up some interesting data! From there I tested my newly discovered theory that there is a common experience and journey taken by anyone who finds themselves thrown into such horrid situations.

The resulting discoveries have clarified my mission: to enable those in the same position to get through the mire faster, more easily and less painfully than I did! For now, let's simply get you acquainted with what I found.

Ten Key Patterns to look out for

There are a number of steps to achieving invisibility and they are so subtle we don't even notice that we are taking them until something extreme happens to shock us back into existence in some way; I certainly didn't notice what had happened and on the surface I was doing just fine. That's also the image I projected to most people; underneath, however, I was slowly disappearing into my own shadow. Many people I speak to can identify with one or more of the areas I have discovered during my journey back. After I realised what was going on with me and I started to look for a way out I understood that first of all I had to be clear on what had gone – where I had gone and why I was no longer me in the truest sense of the word. I was there but not there all at the same time – the real me hiding in plain sight. This is what I found:

When a person has become invisible or is on the way to invisible, the common denominators I found are consistently related to:

- Imbalance: Your life feels as if it's not actually what you thought it was, even if you can't put your finger on exactly what's wrong.

- Image: Keeping up appearances is vitally important, often at the risk of not facing the reality of your situation.

- Identity: You start to question who you are, wondering if you know anymore.

- Individuality: It's easier to fit in than to stand out; your own individuality is suppressed – perhaps to conform or keep the peace.

- Integrity: You accommodate the needs of others at the expense of your own, sacrificing your personal inner integrity in the process.

- Influence: You believe that nobody listens to you anymore and so your opinions do not matter.

- Impact: Apathy sets in; you disengage because there is no point in doing certain things, or perhaps in doing anything at all.

- Imagination: You lose touch with reality as your imagination verges on paranoia. You can't think straight or conceive of a way to change the situation.

- Independence: Unplanned independence throws you into a crisis of vulnerability and confusion; alternatively, you are unable to break free of the circumstances that have enforced your dependency.

- Intuition: You become blind and deaf to the messages of your own intuition and make decisions that are not in your best interests.

There is much to explore around each of these factors. They each have their own subsets and related issues. Together they can be viewed on a spectrum that runs from Completely Invisible to Fully Visible and it is possible to simply assign yourself a number based on your life and how you feel about both your life and yourself. Visibility in this context has absolutely nothing to do with fame or stardom or how many followers you have on social media. Instead, it's about how visible you feel as your true self, whether you are able to live life as you want, be who you want to be in all your uniqueness and how you truly feel about all of that. Each factor can also be considered on its own merits and scored accordingly, to delve deeper into areas that you may want to take a closer look at if you want to change your life. You will also notice that everything in my list begins with I; this is not by design, it is simply how it evolved into the system that I will share and then cover in more detail in subsequent chapters.

Why not have a think about where you are right now. On a scale of 0-10 and thinking overall about your life, who you are and how you show up, how visible and therefore how true to yourself are you right now?

Completely Invisible   **Fully Visible**

0   1   2   3   4   5   6   7   8   9   10

$\longrightarrow$

Does the answer surprise you? Either way, take the next step, a closer look at each aspect and see how they are measuring up in your life right now. Don't worry too much about this exercise, there are no right or wrong answers. Go with what comes up and feels about right for you for most of the time. Consider all aspects of your life. Sometimes it can be a massive wake-up call that things are not quite right. Other times it's just the confirmation that someone needs, indicating exactly what they were thinking but were too afraid to admit to themselves. Finally, be honest with yourself – be careful not to answer what you think you want to hear. That wouldn't serve much purpose at all. If you can't admit the truth even to yourself, then you should definitely keep reading until you can work out what that's all about. Please don't be afraid of exploring who you truly are. It is usually an incredibly uplifting and liberating experience.

Explore your Key Patterns

1. Imbalance

I'm all out of balance   My life is in balance

0   1   2   3   4   5   6   7   8   9   10

2. Image

I hide behind a mask   What you see is
and pretend I'm ok   what you get

0   1   2   3   4   5   6   7   8   9   10

3. Identity

I don't know who I am anymore   I'm totally me

0   1   2   3   4   5   6   7   8   9   10

4. Individuality

I prefer to fit in   **I like to stand out**

0   1   2   3   4   5   6   7   8   9   10

5. Integrity

I tend to go along with others   **I'm true to what I want**

0   1   2   3   4   5   6   7   8   9   10

6. Influence

**I feel that no one
listens to me**   **I share my opinions
without fear**

0   1   2   3   4   5   6   7   8   9   10

7. Impact

**I have no impact
and I've lost interest**   **I'm confident
and engaged**

0   1   2   3   4   5   6   7   8   9   10

8. Imagination

**I can't think straight
most of the time**   **I'm creative
and productive**

0   1   2   3   4   5   6   7   8   9   10

9. Independence

I feel dependent on others   **I am completely independent**

0   1   2   3   4   5   6   7   8   9   10

10. Intuition

I never listen to my Intuition   **I always listen to my Intuition**

0   1   2   3   4   5   6   7   8   9   10

Now add all ten scores to work out the total out of 100.

If you scored between 0 and 69, there's a high probability that you are not where you would like to be right now. There are a number of things that you would like to improve about your life and how you show up in it. You probably feel like you want more control over your own destiny and that it is time you had time for yourself. You want to be able to do the things you have always wanted to do but never had time for. Maybe you would like a change of career to find something you love doing. Perhaps you just want a bit of space, some peace, the ability to breathe deeply and take stock, to tune into yourself. Finding your authentic self is a key step on the road to getting totally real and creating a life you love. Understanding how you hide could create the spark of light that kicks off the reboot.

If you scored between 70 and 89, then things are generally OK in your life but you may be sitting on the fence. The middle ground indicates that things have the potential to shift in either direction. 70 or even 80 out of 100 seems like a good total. It's certainly well over average, more than is required to pass most exams. Even so, it is not quite the complete deal. If it was you would be jumping out of bed *every* day with a great big smile on your face, delighted with every aspect of your life.

What would it take, or what needs to change to nudge you into your best life and your best and truest version of you? You may say to me, hold on a minute, I'm happy here and I don't want to change anything. Then I will ask you, why are you not a 10/10 in each area? What's in the gap? However large or small, my Reboot Protocol will explore that and flush out whatever is in the way of creating your optimum existence. More on that later.

If you scored between 90 and 100, well life must be pretty good, and you feel good about yourself, in control, confident and so on for at least 80% of the time in most situations, and with the majority of the people you find yourself with. All I have to say to you is could anything be better? It's a strange world we live in and I know for a fact that at times it is hard to sustain that 10/10, especially with all the worrying things that are happening out there in the world that we have no control over. Things that still have an impact on our lives and make us question what it's all about. I know I'm not the only one who believes this is all about energy. If we ramp it up high enough and we can sustain this high level we will be operating on a higher frequency, where the very real possibility of our infinite capability to achieve exactly what we want becomes a reality.

How could we change the world in which we are all connected, if more and more of us can move beyond the programming and conditioning that has brought us to this point? Can you imagine a world in love not hate and fear? I can – stay tuned for more information.

"Sometimes being lost is the
best way to find yourself."

L J Vanier

Chapter 3

Imbalance

"...a situation in which two things that should be equal or that are normally equal are not..."

Cambridge Dictionary

"An imbalance occurs when you have too much of some things and too little of others... a lack of balance or a state of disequilibrium."

Vocabulary.com

Imbalance is a fundamental starting point for examining what is going on in your life and whether it feels right or wrong to you. Often people will talk about work-life balance as the main barometer of whether you are living your life as you should, as you want, and if you have time for everything and everyone in it, including yourself. To be honest it doesn't actually matter if you go to work or not, if you are a stay at home mum or even a stay at home dad for that matter, or if you run your own business, are retired, a student, or survive on benefits. At different times of our lives, our circumstances and our priorities change and that is perfectly normal and even expected.

Most new parents can testify to the life-altering capacity of a small human that can inexplicably turn a tidy, organised house into shambolic chaos in a matter of days – even though they slept (or not) for most of the time and in any case were hardly out of their crib! At times like this, imbalance is pretty much a given. Other times though, we are in a routine and all seems well; is it though? Routine can be both the killer of relationships and the outward facing mask that demonstrates all is well. What actually happens when something goes seriously wrong, something that is impossible to hide (for long)? Alternatively, what happens if you simply look at the routine through a different lens? A magnifying glass? A microscope?

The first thing that becomes apparent, maybe, even before we know something really has to change, is that one day everything is fine and then suddenly everything seems out of balance, off-kilter, askew. There may be a calm before the storm, when imperceptible shifts are nudging at your consciousness – the things that you sense but can't quite put your finger on. Then the world turns and you are moving through your life in a fog, where you can't see what's in front of you, sounds are muffled and at the same time there may be a huge roar inside your head that won't go away.

You are feeling your way around to find something solid to hang on to. You probably don't look any different, at least to most people, but your mind and body are hurting inside. No one else can see the feeling in the pit of your stomach, no one hears the voice in your head telling you over and over what you did wrong, what you didn't do, what you should have done. No one feels the weight of your heart, heavy now in your chest, or the effort it takes to breathe, to speak, to put one foot in front of the other and somehow keep going in your life.

Long after the initial sympathy wears off, it all stays with you and there is also anger and fear, guilt, grief, maybe even shame – all locked in a relentless carousel, round and round in your mind as you try to make sense of what has happened or is happening to you. Maybe for the first time in your life you don't know what to do or who to turn to.

Key Pattern 1: IMBALANCE

Suddenly you are no longer in charge of your life and you don't really know who to trust right now. Other clear signs of imbalance are comfort eating, drinking too much, lethargy, duvet days and general lack of interest in anything – at least when you think no one is looking. When someone is looking, or you have to show up, the mask goes on, along with the appropriate clothes and the false smile. In reality it's a coping mechanism that's not really coping at all because behind closed doors it's a very different story. Only your pillow bears witness to the sleepless nights and endless tears.

Take some time out now to contemplate the following:

Q: How is imbalance showing up in your life right now?

The chances are that pretty much everyone will have some degree of imbalance in their life, because after all life is not perfect is it? Sometimes the imbalance is barely there, a shadow formed just out of sight and it takes an event, perhaps something catastrophic such as losing a job, a partner leaving, a parent dying to shock us into the knowledge that actually everything is not all right. It's not all right at all. Maybe it hasn't been right for a long time and the latest happening is simply the one that has tipped the scales. Suddenly with a resounding thud we hit the bottom and we never saw it coming. Or, as we will see later, we just ignored all the warning signs.

Q: What warning signs are you ignoring right now?

If you have identified some warning signs, accept this as a good thing. You are in the right place, among friends. Sometimes just a little nudge is enough to open our eyes to the reality of a situation we have been choosing to ignore. Now you have the perfect opportunity to correct your balance.

"There is no such thing as work-life balance – it is all life.

The balance has to be within you."

Sadhguru

Chapter 4

Image

"…a picture in your mind or an idea of how someone or something is… the way that something or someone is thought of by other people…"

Cambridge Dictionary

"An image is a picture or other representation of a person or thing, or it can be someone's public perception, like a rock star who tries to change his image by dressing like a professor and learning to play chess… Image has its roots in the Latin word imitari, meaning to copy or imitate…"

Vocabulary.com

Consideration of the word image gives rise to a whole variety of definitions that are in range both similar and different, and even contradictory. It's a clever word, a conundrum perhaps, that may help or hinder us. At times the image we portray to the world is not actually how the world perceives us. Often, whatever we do, it may be very difficult to conceal our true self in an effort to be something or demonstrate something that in fact we are not.

If you have ever looked back at old photographs and asked yourself what on earth was I thinking – wearing that outfit, having that haircut, those shoes, that makeup – what did I look like? At the time I bet you thought you were super cool, totally classy, sophisticated, elegant, smart, businesslike or whatever description works best for your specific situation or memory. Can you see now why it didn't work? Is it obvious that you didn't actually portray the image you were looking for? Maybe the colour or style was wrong for you, perhaps the shape or the fit or your choice of accessories. Whatever, it was a costume that you used to create an image of yourself to present yourself to others as you wanted them to see you. The thing with costumes is that it is often apparent to others that this is just a costume. The real you is still right there with flashing lights that everyone but you can see.

People who do not want to draw attention to themselves or feel uncomfortable with how they look often tend to wear neutral colours and hide themselves under baggy clothing so they don't stand out. On the other hand, a life in crisis can also be defined by the keeping up of appearances, pretending everything is all right when you know perfectly well that it isn't. The challenge with being a strong woman who has held it all together for so long – the career, the husband, the kids, the extended family – is that once one of the plates you have been juggling for so long falls and breaks, it is almost a given that one or more of the others crashes around you too.

There may have only been one catastrophic and life-changing event but the chain reaction of aftershocks that it sets in motion are what totally destabilises life as you know it, and what do you do? You run around desperately trying to keep going. Inevitably, unless you stop you will end up surrounded by the debris of what you believed to be your perfectly ordered, in-control life. So, what are the signs of things getting out of control?

An imbalance between your public and private persona. You put on your shiny face and lovely clothes, laughing, smiling and doing what you need to with apparent confidence. Inside however, you are panicking with that whirlwind of emotions and the voice telling you that you are no good. At home you slob about in grubby clothes with unwashed hair, drinking wine, eating chocolate, binge-watching Bridget Jones and anything else that makes you cry.

The inability to say no. It's very important that no one suspects that you are in the state you are in, so you continue to say yes to everything that people ask of you – the fundraiser, the extra work, the financial donations or support… and the cycle continues.

A crazy social life – you know, where the well-meaning friends decide to cheer you up, so you go out too much, eat too much, drink too much. You're the life and soul of the party but you usually end up falling asleep on the sofa when you get home, one last drink in your hand and mascara all over your face. No social life – sometimes you do nothing at all, staying at home, seeing no one, wallowing. When you do venture out this state of affairs is yet again all carefully concealed.

Q: To what extent do you use your image to hide reality?

I have come to the conclusion that often even those who pretend not to care about their appearance actually do. The dressed down, scruffy, no makeup, unkempt look (genuine abject poverty aside) is either a conscious choice or an extreme reaction to a recent traumatic life event. Perpetuated, it may evolve into mental illness or be a symptom of undiagnosed PTSD (Post Traumatic Stress Disorder). Often the ones who pretend not to care about how they look are those who really care the most. A childhood criticism, a teenage slight, a perceived rejection, even a simple misunderstanding creates an emotional reaction; the experience of that emotion, those feelings, are then stored in the neural pathways of the brain as *'the truth'*. People then spend a lifetime compensating for and 'trying' to pretend they don't care about the impact that truth has had. Dig deep enough and there will always be a reason why someone presents themselves to the world as they do.

On the other side of the coin are people who cannot leave the house unless they are immaculately dressed, with full makeup. More extreme still is the current trend even amongst young women to seek out body and facial enhancements; the Botox, lip fillers, extreme eyebrows and lashes deliver more and more unreal images that serve only to mask natural features, often, in my opinion, destroying or at least hiding their original beauty to create an expressionless doll-like façade.

All of this is the expression not of an individual, rather the need to hide individuality, to conform, to look like others, to somehow 'improve' on what is. Each generation and culture throughout history has its extremes of what is considered the fashionable way to appear. Corsets to make the waist appear smaller and the Chinese practice of binding feet are just two examples that spring to mind that illustrate how women (in particular) mutilate their bodies with or without consent in order to hide what they really are to create an image for the benefit of their appearance and standing in the society they belong to or aspire to.

There are very few, if any of us, that have never created some sort of mask, an illusion to hide the way we are feeling, a persona to present to the world that portrays an image we want others to believe of us and that may actually be in conflict with who we are inside, how we are at home behind closed doors. I'm sure that some people will disagree with me on this topic, defending the masks they wear in different situations as their choices, their expression of who they are, their right and so on. They are not wrong and I'm not challenging them; my point is, why do they choose a particular mask? Does it truly reflect who they really are? Some say that you never fully know a person until you live with them and with that I concur, often that's when many take off their masks and we don't like the truth of what they reveal – the person as they really are in their raw state.

I have also experienced a few surprises around not really knowing work colleagues until suddenly being thrust into a team-building event with them. Testing situations often cause the masks to drop and it may not be a pleasant experience. In extreme cases, people who have lived with mass murderers and bigamists are horribly shocked when the truth comes out. Clearly those characters have mastered the art of the mask to disguise their true nature and yet, to some degree, we all use different masks in the different parts of our lives. The various roles we play at work, at home, with family or friends, may all result in us presenting as something or someone different according to who we are with and what our role is in that scenario.

We get so good at this because we are trained virtually from birth to be what others expect of us. Nice girls don't do that, big boys don't cry, you must be brave, be quiet, stop being emotional; I'm sure there are many more you can think of – things that are intentionally about keeping us safe, training us to be in society but also unintentionally teaching us how to hide. Unfortunately, the natural, unique being of unlimited potential that we are born as is gradually eroded; these neural pathways of how to be are constantly reinforced to become our reality and we forget who we truly are and what limitless possibility we actually have.

We also know how to hide. Sadly, because our neural pathways have been strongly created with constant repetition, the resulting behaviour is happening at an unconscious level and that is why we do not even realise what has happened until some life-changing event shocks us out of our slumber. When you find yourself saying things like I don't know who I am anymore, or asking is this all there is to life? that's when you have the opportunity to wake up to the truth of who you could be and to take back control of your life.

I have always been a people watcher – fascinated by what people do, how people look, the ways in which they engage with each other. Sometimes it can be the simplest observations that are the most illuminating and provide insight, even 'Aha' moments when you least expect it. One such example of this happened at a Christmas celebration a few years ago when my thoughts on the masks we wear began to crystallise.

Observations of what's behind the mask

I couldn't help noticing that some of the ladies at this event managed to eat their entire dinner (wonderful Christmas nut roast with all the trimmings followed by sticky toffee pudding and ice cream) and at the end of it their lipstick remained totally in place. There was literally not the slightest smudge, as if it had just been applied. Over the years, I have been given a tip or two: apply, blot, powder, reapply and it should stay put all day. However, whatever the brand and whatever I do, I cannot get my 'lippy' to last beyond the first few mouthfuls – probably not even the welcome drink for that matter!

I got to thinking about this phenomenon and subsequently concluded that this staying power owed nothing to the brand selected, possibly a little more to the rigorous application process, but (from my observations) the most significant influence was directly linked to how these ladies needed to appear and be perceived by the outside world. Let me be clear, there is absolutely no intended criticism of anyone, everyone looked totally lovely and, on the surface, at least, completely in control. I knew, however, that what I was seeing were carefully constructed masks that had to remain in place at all times in order for the wearer to maintain that feeling of control.

I use the word 'feel' here to describe this external appearance, presented to the world in a particular way such that it may hide what is going on beneath the surface – the inner reality of the person that they do not want others to see. The ladies I observed were not particularly well known to me although I had met some of them previously. As I noticed their body language, their expressions, the way they held themselves and interacted with others, and indeed the way they ate their dinners, it became clear that everything they did was carefully orchestrated, organised and consciously presented in such a way to reveal only the elements of themselves that they felt were appropriate for others to see.

This triggered a set of deeper questions: What were they hiding? Was this really them? Were they being authentic? Were the personae I observed reflections of true selves or constructs designed to hide fear and insecurity? I have no clue what fears or insecurities may have been beneath the surface and for the purposes of this book it is not significant, but I knew with absolute certainty that I was seeing 'public' faces and expressions that also revealed the inhibition beneath their careful presentation. I began to wonder about this whole concept.

We live in a challenging world. How often do we put on a mask to create a public face (in whatever way we do this) to hide what is really going on with us, inside of us? Do we do this because we fear we will be judged by others as perhaps not being enough of something? Is that fear of not being enough of something in the eyes of another exactly what holds us back in life? What does our fear of what others think say about what is really going on for us? Who is our public face really for? Is it us or them? Sometimes we use it as armour, our protection, but what if the very means we use to protect ourselves actually creates blockages for us as well? Of course, harm as we perceive it may not be able to penetrate our defences and yet, as with every barrier we create, the nature of that barrier is just as strong a defence against good, even against love perhaps.

Protection carefully applied can be an impermeable shield against all forces. The construction is so expertly created on a framework of fear (founded or otherwise) that it is entirely possible to become isolated in our perceptions of what might be, rather than what actually is! Fear defines us if we let it and then who we are meant to be becomes simply the shadow behind the mask. Every day we all create our own masks, our own defences, our own ways of hiding from the world. As we do this, the sad reality is that we are smothering our authenticity, our true self. Because of our fears we do not live as who we are meant to be. If we are not who we are meant to be then we cannot love ourselves. If we cannot love ourselves then by definition we are living in fear and not love. When we live in love, the possibilities are limitless and only then can we attract what we are looking for.

I think it is time to look behind the mask.

Key Pattern 2: IMAGE

Colour becomes the new black

So, you may be thinking that I went straight from that moment in the mirror to getting it all together and getting ME back; however, that was simply the turning point or should I say the major turning point. There were many twists in the tale before I got to a point where it all made sense and I just knew what was going on, what had happened, how I got out of it and what I needed to do to help you do the same (or even not go there at all!).

After that turning point, I set up a business doing what I love and what I do well. Days were spent agonising over the name, a website was built, cards were printed and off I went. I got some great clients and thought I was on my way. With hindsight the fit wasn't exactly right. Don't get me wrong, I love helping people sort out the processes in their business and I am very good at it and yet something was always niggling away at me, something that told me this wasn't quite right.

Eventually it hit me: I was still wearing my corporate clothes, literally the black, the grey, the navy – all the colours and styles that contributed towards making me invisible. Of course, we all know by now that this was not who I was – who I am. Getting back into colour, and the right colours for me for that matter, was a huge boost to my confidence and there are many to thank on this part of the journey.

One voice resonated loud and clear at this point, that of my son. I can still hear him clearly pointing out that I nearly always wore black, he didn't like me in black and it made me look 'witchy'. Expressed in such a way that I knew he was thinking about the wicked witch rather than the good one! Hmm, not how you want your children to perceive you, even grown-up children. There is something about wearing the right clothes in the right colours that does things for your self-esteem and confidence and this was the first glimmer of hope in the journey to find myself.

As far as the business was concerned, the problem of the corporate look is that, as this was not me, I was not projecting an authentic picture of who I was. The fit was not right and as we all know, people buy people and they have a sixth sense for finding you out.

Funny how I had spent over 25 years attempting to fit squarely into the corporate world, which as we know is full of round holes. My edges, the parts that made me different, had been rounded off and so I slid into my allotted space and became invisible. Now here I was out of this place but still projecting that same image… DOH! No wonder it didn't feel right.

Changing my image was just another starting point in what would become a huge, random puzzle of pieces that didn't seem to fit together properly. 'All the King's horses and all the King's men couldn't put Humpty together again' and at times it seemed as if I was to suffer the same fate as poor Humpty and be lost and broken forever. Then I had another of those blinding flash moments: this is not something that can be fixed from the outside, this has to come from within! And guess what, as soon as I had worked that out I started seeing confirmation everywhere including this lovely quote found on the Internet:

"If an egg is broken by an outside force, life ends.

If an egg is broken by an inside force, then life begins.

Great things happen from the inside."

Anonymous

"Always be a first-rate version of yourself instead of a second-rate version of somebody else."

Judy Garland

Chapter 5

Identity

"...who a person is, or the qualities of a person or group that make them different from others..."

Cambridge Dictionary

"Your identity is what makes you 'you'. If you are having 'an identity crisis', then I guess you can't figure out who you are... the individual characteristics by which a thing or person is recognised or known..."

Vocabulary.com

Whoever you are, the image you present represents your identity and this is the reason you fight so hard to maintain that image. For example, you are daughter, wife, mother, boss and more. Sometimes different people see a different side of us: our family may see a different person from our colleagues or subordinates – or maybe they don't. It doesn't really matter, because inside ourselves, however we present ourselves to different groups, their responses to us are what validates our identity. When they love us, want us, need us, we own that identity and subsequently define ourselves by it and through it. Inevitably, when change occurs a chunk of our identity is also torn away.

When a life-changing event happens – a bereavement, a break-up, a redundancy, a rejection or departure – it is almost impossible not to take it personally. We apportion blame to ourselves and think if we had done something differently the outcome would be different, and we would not be where we are now. The problem is with any kind of loss or rejection where we have invested some of ourselves, we have hooked our identity to that person or situation.

It is very hard to suddenly have to deal with, for example, not being a wife or an employee or not being needed as mum when the kids have left home. As we get older it would seem that these changes can often tumble into each other creating a domino effect. Before we know it all the dominos are fallen. Then I hear: What now? Who am I? Is this all there is?

The heartbreaking reality is that so many (usually) women experience one or more huge events in their lives after which they are left reeling in shock and often numb for a while because suddenly everything they thought they knew has become destabilised. The identity (or identities) they have intrinsically woven through their life is no longer necessary and may well have been taken away suddenly, without permission. I said it myself and have heard it said by so many others since, "I don't know who I am anymore."

When your reference point is gone and with it a huge part of your identity, it's hard to remember who you were before and even harder to know how to be now.

Q: How has your identity been affected?

If you are asking yourself who you are, not recognising the person you see in the mirror every morning, it can be extremely stressful to get through the day. When it feels that all your hopes and dreams have been dashed and there is nothing to look forward to, what can you do to make things better? The first question I ask is: "Who do you want to be?" then, "What do you want to do?" From there we go on a journey to discover what makes you YOU! This usually throws up a few surprises. Once you start exploring things below the surface a whole new world opens up and the colour comes back. A birthday trip to the theatre unexpectedly drove this message home.

"Sometimes standing out is the best way to fit in"

It was a great lesson unexpectedly conveyed in the fabulous West End musical *Kinky Boots*. I am not entirely sure what I was expecting from such a flamboyant musical theatre production, however it wasn't an eye-opening confirmation of one of the fundamental principles of the Totally Real, Totally You approach. Standing out to fit in hit me in a very precise way: this is exactly one of the messages I have been investigating for the last few years. It's a huge part of reclaiming your true self, in order to live an authentic life as who you are meant to be. It took a drag queen in a sparkly dress and vertiginously high-heeled boots in a London theatre to prompt me to speak out a little more on the subject.

Right now, you might be thinking the whole concept of a drag queen standing up for who they really are has no relevance to you whatsoever. I say exactly the opposite. Granted, it may be an extreme example, however my view is that to a greater or lesser degree we can all relate to something in this story. My own personal experience concerns a work situation – one in which I felt unheard and largely invisible in a particular group of people, in spite of holding a significant management role with high visibility and responsibility in the wider organisation.

So, what was my solution to this situation? After looking around at my colleagues, my response was to adopt the same corporate uniform as everyone else – the suits in navy, black and grey, typical of that world and in colours that do me no favours at all. This was corporate attire at its best. It didn't come cheap but it simply wasn't me! What I didn't realise at the time was the more I struggled to fit in with everyone else, the more invisible I actually became.

Looking back with hindsight is easy, but it is only with this retrospective view that I can see that all the effort of fitting in simply hid the real me. Consequently, my real visibility, impact and influence was negligible, especially in terms of achieving the support required to succeed in a role that focused on creating change and promoting innovation. You can imagine that this did not bode well.

Regardless of the personal insecurities and dented confidence, I gave great presentations, exceeded every target I was ever given, and delivered award-winning projects that saved millions of pounds. Still nobody noticed either me or my results. The more I achieved, the less they noticed and often my successes were claimed by or attributed to others. On one occasion after months of meticulous research and data collection my findings were simply stonewalled with an unbelievable, "I don't believe you." Imagine the frustration! While this particular exchange signalled the beginning of the end of this era in my life, for a while I soldiered on with my desperate attempts at being corporate until inevitably I had all but disappeared into the background of my own existence and reached the point of no return.

I have been working on myself and for myself ever since. Each new revelation is a lesson in what happened and a marker for what can never happen again. Day by day, I see ever more clearly every way in which I allowed my essence, my truth, my *self* to be subjugated, suppressed and almost (but not quite) totally squashed. I share this part of my journey now as I am hearing the same story over and over, frequently seeing how others are going through similar experiences to mine – observing the many ways that people hide in plain sight.

Everyone has the capacity to adopt a chameleon-like approach. We all have the ability to change who we are to fit in with whatever is around us. Eventually, we get so good at camouflage that we forget who we really are. Our thoughts, our words and even what we look like is no longer a true reflection of our individual potential and uniqueness.

Key Pattern 3: IDENTITY

So, what's the message? My own experiences and the *Kinky Boots* narrative clearly indicate that in order to fit in, to get the attention, the respect, the love we crave, we have to do the exact opposite of what we perceive as the obvious route. If you attempt to fit in, you will not stand out at all. You can eventually make yourself completely invisible and actually repel what you are moving towards. So how do I justify this stance? It's easy really, because on a subliminal level, we humans are generally very perceptive and somehow we can pick up a level of dishonesty, a lack of integrity, a sense of something not quite right and we respond accordingly.

In reality, the response would be pretty accurate because if you are not being you it will be apparent in some way that you are hiding something; others will respond to that with a lack of trust towards you and the cycle begins. I don't know if we give off different pheromones or something like that, because I'm not convinced that this even takes place on the conscious level. Once it has begun, however, the slide into invisibility is often achieved without us even noticing and we may reside there in all innocence unless something happens to shock us out of complacency and into awareness.

My mission is to wake people up to the knowledge of their own brand of awesomeness that belongs to them and no one else. To demonstrate what is possible when you decide to embrace who you really are. Being you in all your glory, in all your faults, in whatever attire you choose to wear, with whatever views you can claim as your own, with however you choose to behave, however you engage with others in all aspects of your life. That my friends is how you will stand out – how you will shine.

When you truly shine through, that is when you will attract what you are looking for: people will trust you, they will be drawn to you, you will love them and they will love you. You will belong, you will fit in and stand out at the same time, because you are as you are meant to be – different, unique, honest and truthful. You will allow people to know you and you will no longer be afraid of showing who that is because standing out is fitting in! This sentiment was also attributed to Dr Seuss who apparently said, "Why fit in when you were born to stand out?" Certainly, this was part of his philosophy, but apparently he never uttered these exact words!

Always remember: it's good to be real, it's great to be you, and it's life-changing when you can really be you – Totally You! It is also prudent to listen to your intuition in respect of how those around you are impacting your ability to be yourself. Even the most evil psychopaths will often reveal themselves eventually, and while the films dwell on serial killers, not all psychopaths are that evil. It's actually pretty likely that you may have come across some psychopaths in your own life.

According to inc.com, they are actually quite common in the corporate world. If you are not quite sure how to spot a psychopath, www.discovermagazine.com produced a helpful checklist in 2016. Just a few of the traits they mention include glibness/superficial charm, grandiose sense of self-worth, need for stimulation/proneness to boredom, pathological lying, conning/manipulation, lack of remorse/guilt, shallow affect, callousness/lack of empathy, parasitic lifestyle, promiscuous sexual behaviour. If you can identify too many psychopaths around you, their clever manipulation may well be detrimental to your identity as they control how you can respond and behave in their orbit.

People will instinctively know when you are hiding and that is potentially why you don't always get the reaction from others (especially in work situations) that you anticipated. When the identity you present to the world is authentic and beyond the control of manipulative others, that's when other people will see you and they will respond accordingly. More than likely this will be completely different from how they usually behave towards you.

"Most people are other people. Their thoughts are someone else's opinions, their lives a mimicry, their passions a quotation."

Oscar Wilde

Chapter 6

Individuality

"...the qualities that make a person or thing different from others..."

Cambridge Dictionary

"Whether it's eating breakfast for lunch, learning Celtic step dancing, building birdhouses from popsicle sticks, showing off your shark tattoo, or speaking with an Australian accent on Tuesdays, all of these things can express your individuality, meaning what makes you unique... the sum total of characteristics that make up a particular individual. Individuality consists of the good, the bad – and even the crazy – that make a person distinct."

Vocabulary.com

If your identity is what you present to the world that makes you different from others, then individuality is the measure of how different. Your own particular idiosyncrasies – how you dress, the way you do your hair and makeup. We all have them. They are the expression of our individuality. Often when idiosyncrasy is used in a description of someone it generally conjures up an image of eccentricity – the clichéd cat lady or the old lady dressed in purple. What it doesn't do is identify that actually every human on the planet is highly individual. I love the breakdown of the word idiosyncrasy from the original Greek that demonstrates this more clearly – that which is our own is all mixed up together. The implication being that because it is our own, the mix will always be different.

Of course, we share DNA, genes, looks that may go back generations but ultimately we are all different. We all have our own views or feelings and ways of behaving. How much of this is, however, what we are born with and how much is a product of our circumstances or upbringing? There are countless studies that look at the impact of society on behaviour, and others that can show similarities between siblings or twins that were separated at birth or an early age and brought up in different areas even different countries or cultures.

You may also recall the television series produced by Granada Television that began with *7 Up*, talking to seven-year-old children from different backgrounds and different parts of the UK. This series has followed these individuals every seven years and *63 Up* premiered in 2019. It is a fascinating insight that shows the opinions, beliefs and wishes of seven-year-old children brought together as a group but representative of diverse socio-economic backgrounds. The programme invites us to consider whether what was shown in the first episode was indicative of what followed. One cannot help but wonder whether the lives of these individuals would have taken the same course had they not had their lives under the spotlight and moments of fame every seven years.

Certainly, the backlash from a press campaign against him following opinions aired in one episode impacted one of the participants quite significantly. Yet another chose to drop out after an argument with the producer. Were the adults they became the adults they were always destined to be or did the publicity surrounding the series play a huge part in how they presented themselves as time progressed? Were their choices at least in part made as a result of knowing they would soon be in the public eye again and therefore because they wanted to impress? They cannot fail to have been significantly impacted. The pressure to either live up to their early privileged expectations or overcome their poor social background must have been huge. I can only speculate that the pressure to do what they had very publicly stated aged seven may have restrained them in some way from expressing their true individuality. This may have taken them down a very different path, resulting in a completely different story.

Individuality, or lack of it, is the pattern that usually becomes apparent when you start asking who you are, it is the sign that keeps flashing in your head – the one that says you are nobody. You see, somewhere on this journey to the present day, your individuality has disappeared, or you have chosen not to hold on to it. The things that make you YOU, or the things you might have chosen to do, have been overwritten by the demands of others, whoever those others are. The need to fit in, the desire to please, to conform, to be superwoman, or even just to cope with the daily logistics of family, work and life means that your own zest for life and passions have been put aside or forgotten. It becomes far less about who you are and much more about doing and being what is expected of you. Playing the appropriate role or roles that carve up the different aspects of your life.

The irreverence of your inner child and love of silly things is often suppressed, as things get serious for you at work or as a parent. It becomes almost impossible to do anything impulsive or impromptu as you are tied by the constraints of the various roles you play. You may have learned that if you do something impulsive or out of the ordinary, others will judge you as weird or worse, or wonder why you are behaving out of character. Never mind that that character has been assigned by them, even if you have accepted the part. There comes a point where you have no idea how to do anything else because you have completely forgotten the individual who used to do those different things and the crazy social life that may follow a break-up is not really you either.

Over the years you have created an image consistent with the treadmill of your life, and maintaining that image now means you won't draw any attention to yourself. Is it really you, or is it a construct designed to create the camouflage you need in the world(s) you inhabit? Do you wear clothes that help you to fit in rather than stand out and express yourself? What about having different ideas or opinions from those around you? Do you express what you really believe or want, or do you just go along with everyone else? If you find yourself questioning the very essence of who you are, then maybe it is time to question who you're meant to be. When we find ourselves discarded from relationships or displaced from a job, the time has come to examine exactly what constraints we have allowed others to place around us.

Q: In what ways have you permitted your individuality to be dimmed?

Each of us is born as a unique combination of cells with a unique capacity to be as individual as our biology and physiology determines. Even identical twins with the same DNA have their differences and over time this may become more apparent according to how they progress through life – what they eat, the jobs they do, where they live, who they interact with and so on. They may be different heights, weights, have different abilities and interests, and also different susceptibility to illness and disease. My own twin cousins are a clear example of this. They had the same upbringing, went to the same church and schools. They were initially exposed to the same influences and also experienced the same positive events and the same tragedies. Later, however, they made their own choices at various stages of their lives: friends, college, university, professions, interests to name but a few. Today it is still obvious they are brothers but they are dissimilar in many ways – each with their own strengths and weaknesses with a completely different outlook on many things. Nor do they look like the clichéd 'peas in a pod' of their early years.

The question this raises is quite simple. If twins are able to command their own individuality, why do so many of us spend our lives emulating others, trying to fit in and sometimes allowing our own individuality to be subsumed by the people we associate with and the circumstances we put ourselves in?

Key Pattern 4: INDIVIDUALITY

Before the indignation rises and you begin to resist the acknowledgement of free will and your own freedom of choice in relation to the people around you and the specific circumstances of your life, please take a deep breath and pause for a moment. Disregard (for now) your early life, your parents, the kind of upbringing you experienced and so on. Thinking about right now, this very moment in time and ask yourself:

- Do I freely choose the people who are around me on a regular basis?

- How have I created the current situation of my life?

- Is this what I truly want?

If your answers suggest that you do not freely choose those around you, that you believe that in part or in full your current situation is not of your own making and that what you have is not what you really want at all, it's time to take some responsibility. There are always choices available to you even in the most extreme of circumstances. Unless you have been abducted and held captive against your will in some way, recognise that however today's situation has been arrived at, on some level you have chosen those around you. You have had choices available to you and you made choices along the way.

History and literature are full of examples of how slaves or those held captive have made choices about how to deal with the situation in which they find themselves. Choices that were often about holding on to a sense of self, of who they really were, whether this was held inside with a huge capacity of inner strength and refusal to be broken, or shouted aloud in defiance of being owned and controlled. Two examples come to mind. The first, in relation to prisoners of war, the second, a tale of slavery.

I once had the privilege to interview a number of veterans who had survived being held captive in Burma. Decades after their barbaric incarceration and horrific treatment, these men all told me there were no words in any language to explain what had actually happened to them. What they did share with me, as their families told me later, was more than they had ever been able to put into words before. Maybe being of an age that they were finally facing their own mortality helped or maybe I was somehow the intended channel for their message. Who knows?

Finally, another two decades on, I am able to make some sense of what I was told and align it with the context of this book. I asked each of them how they had managed to survive against all odds, when so many others didn't make it out alive. What they told me was uncannily consistent, however, it is in no way a suggestion that those who died were not at least attempting to adopt the same tactics. There were far too many other factors in the mix – debilitating illness, starvation, beating and random killing are the most often mentioned and any of these could mean the end for even the most resolute. What these proud old men shared has stayed with me all these years – they knew who they were, they held on to their sense of self, the essence of their individuality at the core of their being. It gave them strength and they refused to give up or give in. Like those liberated from the concentration camps in Europe, these men were walking skeletons – emaciated shadows of their former selves when they were finally liberated. We can only be humbled by knowing how they held on to what was at the very core of their being and somehow this aided their survival.

The grandfather of my friend Kate, the late Stan Sentance, also survived a Japanese prisoner of war camp. The hapless Stan by virtue of getting on the wrong ship at the wrong time ended up in the notorious Changi camp in Singapore. Somehow, he survived beatings, near starvation and tropical disease to emerge weighing just 5½ stone (77lbs/35kg) and eventually made it back home to

Hampshire where he lived in Titchfield, the village of his birth, until he died aged 93 on 19 December 2002.

I am not going to repeat here the horrors of what Stan went through or the life-changing (but not visibly apparent) injuries that he was left with. Beatings had left him profoundly deaf – one can barely imagine the rest. I simply want to pay homage to an irrepressible individual. Stan was the epitome of a unique human being – a huge character housed in a small frame, with a twinkling eye and a great sense of humour. I knew Stan for the last few years of his life and like those other POWs who had been in Burma, he too had held on to his self-belief and knowledge of exactly who he was.

A young Stan Sentance before the war

There was no compromise with Stan and he remained stubborn to the end. One time he was in hospital and refusing food because he declared that if he was going to die, he wanted to die at home. The hospital sent him home together with the information that he was unlikely to die of starvation because his body had gone into survival mode after what he went through during his incarceration and that it knew how to do it again. The added bonus was they also found some tropical bugs or bacteria that had been in his system for nearly 60 years and they were not likely to kill him either.

A creature of habit, Stan would have a couple of drinks at a local hostelry in the evening and even when he could no longer walk down the road he refused to enter or leave the building in his wheelchair. In the last few weeks of his life he only made a few visits and then one night I got a call to say Stan wanted to go out that evening and would like to see me. He found it difficult to tip up a glass to drink and as the evening progressed, we resorted to smaller glasses with his last sips from a shot glass.

At the end of an evening filled with the usual banter and much hilarity it was finally time to leave and, as usual, he insisted on dancing out. Stan loved to dance – even when barely able to walk, he always wanted to dance a few steps. Somehow, with me holding the old man up and others poised to catch us, we managed to twirl around a couple of times and exit gamely through the doors to where his wheelchair waited.

That was Stan's swansong – an exit on his terms. He passed away in his own home later that night with his son at his side. Nothing he had gone through had ever taken away the core of this man and he remained an individual and true to himself to the very end. I am proud and honoured to have known Stan. My hope is that by sharing just a glimpse of his story it will serve to demonstrate just exactly how resilient we humans can be. To shine a light on how important it is to hold on to our individuality and more importantly just how difficult it is for someone to take it away from us, unless of course we let them.

Q: How does this story make you feel about your own individuality right now?

The second example that I referred to earlier comes from the novel *Roots: The Saga of an American Family* by Alex Haley. Although accompanied by controversy about the historical accuracy of this tale due to inconsistencies in dates, names and slave records, Haley claims to be a direct descendant of Kunta Kinte, the Mandinka tribesman captured in the Gambia as a teenager, sold into slavery and the key character of his book. The actual events and conversations in the story may well be fiction, however the way it continues to draw our interest leads me to believe in the validity of the historical narrative.

The sentiment that comes through loud and clear, expressing exactly what I am referring to, is the concept of ancestry and knowing who you are, where you come from and what that means. In this case Kunta Kinte is the Mandinka warrior and the traditional baby-naming ceremony passed orally through the generations confers both the individual name of the baby and all of the characteristics and associations of the chosen name together with those of the ancestors and the attributes of the Mandinka tribe.

The huge importance given to a name by the tribe is illustrated when Kunta Kinte is renamed Toby by his new 'owners'. He steadfastly insists that he is Kunta Kinte, refusing to answer to the name Toby even when he is whipped almost to death. Each time he is asked, "What is your name?" he screams out, "I am Kunta Kinte," and is whipped some more. Eventually bleeding profusely and barely conscious, he understands that this is a pointless way to die, he whispers for the benefit of the slave owners that his name is Toby. Inside his head, however, he never gives up on his true belief and his real name – the name that makes him the individual that he is. This name and the lineage with which it is associated is then passed into the oral tradition and conferred on the next generation as the newborns are given their own name.

So, what's in a name then? Is our name an intrinsic part of who we are as individuals? What's important? Is there any significance to the name we adopt when we get married? Different cultures have different traditions: the woman keeps her father's name, the woman takes her husband's name, both original surnames are combined in either order with associated different meanings, sometimes everyone keeps their original birth name. There are now so many different permutations of what is acceptable and there could be a whole debate on what happens in respect of any particular choice.

The only purpose to mentioning this is to highlight what impact the name(s) we are known by may have on different aspects of our life – possibly our energy, how we feel about ourselves and how in turn this may impact on our senses of our own individuality. After being divorced for many years I have recently gone back to my birth name, Elizabeth Carney, after 30 years with my married surname. It makes sense to me anyway. It feels like there has been a palpable energy shift and a release back to who I really am. I am Totally Me again having come full circle to the beginning of new and infinite possibilities.

My sister on the other hand never changed her name when she got married and of all the people I know she has always been one of the clearest on exactly who she is and always has been. I have several friends who have taken the surnames of several husbands meaning they have changed their name three or four times. I am curious to the impact on an individual on multiple name changes. How important is it? Do individuals change with a name? What happens when you are no longer associated with the person who gave you that name? Does your individuality get eroded, diminished by that broken association, or can you hold on to who you truly are?

How do diminutives or other variations on our name impact us? Is this an indication of how others perceive us? If we answer to what people call us even if that is not what we really want to be known as, are we again suppressing our individuality?

I have a friend called Debby and that is her name and exactly how it is spelled. I think her husband may get away with calling her Debs but that's about it. I remember one occasion where she was most indignant (and rightly so) because someone insisted on calling her Deborah. It took several attempts before the individual concerned finally accepted what her name was and that it had never been Deborah. It might have been simpler not to bother going through this with a relative stranger but I was quite proud of her for standing her ground and knowing exactly who she is and for her zero-tolerance policy on the matter.

The name Elizabeth clearly has many shortened versions: Liz, Lizzie, Liza, Beth, Betty and more, and for most of my life I have always answered to Liz or Elizabeth. Dad was the only person really allowed to call me Lizzie although my brother would call me Little Lizzie or Betty if he wanted to be particularly irritating.

I believe that how we choose to be known and what we allow others to call us is significant in respect of how we see ourselves and how we want to portray who we are to the world. Take the name Tony for example: I don't think I have never known a Tony that wasn't a really personable, likeable, cheery character and most of them have said at one time or another that when they were called Anthony as a child, they knew they were in trouble. That's my experience of many people who are only known by the shortened version of their name.

Then of course there are the stage names adopted by musicians, singers and actors the world over, sometimes by design, often by accident. A June 2020 article by Megan Decker and Jennifer Algoo (harpersbazaar.com) discusses celebrities that do not use their real names. The stories behind the names offer some fascinating insights. I'm not going to go into detail here but in each of the following examples a new identity was created and from there the individuality that we now associate with each of these names evolved. These people are now, or were their name, becoming in the process of transition something they were not before.

- Marilyn Monroe was baptised Norma Jeane Baker and that was already her second surname. She dropped the surname of her first husband because a studio executive thought people wouldn't be able to pronounce it and she suggested Monroe because it was a family name on her mother's side. He then dubbed her Marilyn because she reminded him of someone else.

- Bono grew up as Paul Hewson and apparently adopted his new name after a local hearing aid shop called Bonovox.

- David Bowie was born David Jones, and because of The Monkees changed his stage name from Davy Jones to David Bowie allegedly after the knife and its inventor of the same name.

- Bob Dylan was born Robert Zimmerman but adopted his new name in homage to poet Dylan Thomas.

- Sting became the stage name of Gordon Sumner after he wore a black and yellow striped sweater for a gig with the Phoenix Jazzmen and has been Sting ever since.

- Natalie Portman was born Nete-Lee Herslag in Israel but on emigrating to the United States the family changed the surname to Portman, the actress's maternal grandmother's maiden name, and Neta-Lee became Natalie.

- Helen Mirren was born Ilyena Lydia Mironoff but her father changed the family's last name from Mironoff to Mirren. Ilynea then simplified her first name to Helen when she embarked on her acting career.

- John Legend is the stage name of John Roger Stephens. John Legend was the nickname his friends started calling him that grew into his stage name when more people knew him by that name than his real name. Legend explained in an MTV interview that he decided to "…just go for it. People are going to pay attention and I'm going to either live up to my name or I'm not," he added. "My bet was on me trying to live up to the name."

The rest as they say is history!

Our names may define us or we may choose to be defined by them, or reject them totally and create ourselves as a new character with a new name. Our individual character is a core indicator of who we are and clearly demonstrates that we are able to function in a separate existence from anyone else. Why then do so many of us suppress our own individuality, often as a means of appeasing others and as a consequence denying our undeniable right to be unique? One only has to look at gangs and music subcultural groups (mods, punks, rockers etc) to find a need to conform and be the same as others rather than to stand out and be an individual.

It has always been a source of bemusement to see the sometime rebels, who often start on this path as a means of expressing their own individuality, become submerged and insignificant as they merge into invisible, faceless members of the collective. They dress the same, walk the same, talk the same and to be honest it is rather boring. Many of these groups serve teenagers and there is some safety in rebelling in numbers rather than alone and there is also the emotional connection of belonging to something at a difficult stage of development. People do transition from this stage completely, however some seem to find it impossible to move on and remain stuck forever in the safety of their cocoon, unable to spread their wings further. Others move on to other groups to fill their need for acceptance – social, college, work and religious examples come to mind.

I am not suggesting that there is anything wrong with belonging to groups, and of course we all need affirmation and acceptance from our peers and other parts of society with which we interact. I highlight this aspect of our human behaviour to illustrate how, especially when engaging at extreme ends of the spectrum, it is entirely possible to become totally consumed by the ideas and values of a group to the extent we may find ourselves and therefore our individuality completely suppressed.

This need for collectiveness is not, however, restricted to teenage gangs and the more outrageous groups, it can be seen in all aspects of society. Paratroopers for example, marines or any other group of service personnel that have trained together, served together and maybe have seen combat together tend to have a shared language that excludes others but also a code and a connection that stays with them long past their service days. I have observed immense pride, mutual respect, sticking together, and always looking out for each other.

There is also the secret language and of course the secrets never spoken. They move on to many different walks of life, new jobs and careers; however, when they reunite the old rules of engagement return and the pack tend to prevail over the individuals. The armed forces clearly need to operate as tight units, generally without maverick individuality (despite what the films would have us believe); what is interesting is how that group functionality is so easily rekindled.

Shared experience does not always have to lead to suppression of individuality; my school reunions are evidence of a range of highly individual women who have achieved in many different areas. Women who are mothers and grandmothers now, married, divorced, gay and straight who have forged their own path but every five years or so get together to celebrate the time we shared. We simply pick up where we left off and, to a degree, we know each other so well. I don't think we were ever a collective, other than attending the same school at the same time. We were always individuals and encouraged to be so. I am sure that there are some that may have lost sight of that quality at times and the regular reunions serve to remind us of our uniqueness as well as our shared history. Funny that 40-plus years on, there is still a pull and still a connection but we marvel at all the different things we have been and who we have become – and yet our characters are instantly recognisable no matter how long we have lived our separate existences.

But what if you can no longer see your own individuality? What if a group mentality or submission to a controlling other has left you afraid to speak out, to put forward your own ideas or even to know that you may have valuable and constructive ideas of your own? What if you suppress your instincts to be unique and different because you do not wish to stand out and you want to fit in? Do you go along with what others want just to keep the peace, to keep them happy? What if knowing that you have done this now makes you uncomfortable? What do you now see or feel? Just knowing is the first step in seeing that there is an alternative and that suppressing your individuality is another step on the road to the real you being totally invisible.

"The individual has always had
to struggle to keep from being
overwhelmed by the tribe.

If you try it, you will be lonely often,
and sometimes frightened.

But no price is too high to pay for the
privilege of owning yourself."

Friedrich Nietzsche

Chapter 7

Integrity

"The quality of being honest and having strong moral principles that you refuse to change... the quality of being whole and complete..."

Cambridge Dictionary

"Having integrity means doing the right thing in a reliable way. It's a personality trait that we admire, since it means a person has a moral compass that doesn't waver. It literally means 'wholeness' of character, just as an integer is a 'whole number' with no fractions. Physical objects can have integrity too – if you're going over a rickety old bridge that sways in the wind, you might question its structural integrity."

Vocabulary.com

It is a sad but true observation that when you are unable to be true to who you really are, you have no inner integrity. This does not mean you are a dishonest person; it simply means that your personal integrity has disappeared as you do the bidding of others. Work, kids, partner, friends – all their needs take precedence over yours and you find that you place little value on yourself or having some me time. You lose sight of what it really is that you want because you are so busy accommodating the demands of everyone else in your world. You find it hard to think of yourself and even harder to say no.

As a mum I know just how easy it is to get sucked into the world of doing anything and everything for your child. Even if being a parent was your greatest dream, nothing prepares you for what happens when a child arrives and all ideas of juggling parenthood and everything else you wanted have simply evaporated. You constantly tell yourself that it doesn't matter anymore but let's be honest here, as much as you love your children, sometimes it does matter. Sometimes something happens that makes you realise that, actually, you also matter. Now it is time to take care of you instead of everybody else.

If you recognise that you have been fooling yourself all along and there are things that you would rather do, hopes and dreams that you would still like to fulfil, then it's time to find a way to make them come true. If you think about who you really are for a moment, are you happy that who you are right now is truly you, or have you settled into something less than *you*? Are you going to be a victim about it and blame everyone else in your life or are you going to step up and take responsibility? Understanding that our own choices contribute to any situation we find ourselves in is a key starting point to enable us to reboot and start afresh with the operating system of our own inner integrity.

Q: Where in your life are you not being true to yourself?

I have heard it said that one of the greatest regrets that people have in later life is being what others want them to be rather than being themselves. Hands up if you have ever felt like this at any stage in your life. I will bet that you can probably remember at least one occasion where when you look back you wish that you had stood up for what you really wanted to be or do. Perhaps you still can, or more likely it is no longer possible for any number of reasons – the people you were with are no longer around, the place has gone, the law has changed – it could be anything but you still wish deep down that you had followed your own path rather than one mapped out for you by well-meaning parents, friends or others in your sphere of influence.

Not being who you want to be because others want or expect you to be something/somebody different is an incremental stage of becoming invisible and significantly is about not being true to yourself and therefore compromising your personal integrity.

Key Pattern 5: INTEGRITY

When I use integrity in this context, I am not questioning your morality or your honesty or suggesting that you might be a bad person in any way. I am referring to your internal barometer, your truthfulness with yourself. The soundness and wholeness of what makes you who you are will always be diminished when you deny yourself what you really want. I am sure there will be some who will make a case for how circumstances were against them, they didn't have the money to do it, they didn't want to upset somebody – the list goes on (watch the film *Pursuit* of *Happyness* with Will Smith before you make those types of assertions again!). Nor am I suggesting that it is right to go around upsetting people or insisting that you always get your own way – it's not that at all.

You can be the most upstanding model citizen, friend, family member, parent, whatever, who 'always does the right thing in a reliable way' – you are considered whole, wholesome maybe, yet if you have simply adopted this persona for a quiet life, to keep others happy, you may appear to have excellent external integrity, but your internal integrity is in shreds. More than likely you have got so used to acting in such a way, and your own dreams are so far in the past that they have been forgotten and you no longer even remember yourself.

Habitual liars believe their own fabrications to be true as a result of the intricate web of deceit they spin around their every interaction. They are found out when they forget something, or when different people compare notes; sometimes they even leave a deliberate trail so they are discovered. At the point of discovery, they are exposed for who they really are. I expect sometimes that must be a relief – perhaps I have just read too many crime novels!

So, on the surface there you are doing the right thing in a reliable way. You are the good girl, the pacifier, the one everyone can rely on to sort things out, the one who never says no, the good egg. You are reliable, honest, sound as a pound. You are all of those things and many more, however you are also none of those things – not you, not the real you. The real you may be inside screaming in frustration to be let out. The real you may get that sinking feeling in your stomach when your colleague or your boss comes over (usually on Friday afternoon) and says (again!), "I've got to leave now but this has to be finished today – I know you won't mind staying and finishing it off for me." The version of you sitting at your desk who minutes ago was looking forward to a relaxing soak in the bath followed by lounging around in front of the telly with a take-away and a bottle of wine smiles and says, "Of course not, I'll make sure it's done."

You instantly find yourself clutching a bulging file of messy paperwork, staring at their hastily departing back, wishing that for once you had the guts to stand up for yourself and say no. Or perhaps the real you is so buried that you don't even notice. Has the real you become so detached that it doesn't even recognise that you are acting in contradiction to what you really want or feel? Has your inner integrity turned into a rickety old bridge that you can't rely on because you haven't maintained it? If you are always true to yourself first, the truth will shine from you and the right people will be attracted to you.

If you are in the habit of 'lying' to yourself regardless of how you appear externally to others then your internal integrity is like that rickety old bridge. You have no structural integrity or in this case you could be described as having no backbone. As I wrote this paragraph the following example popped up in my Facebook feed and illustrates exactly what I am talking about:

A valuable lesson this

M (Husband) – Is there anything I can do?

S (Wife) – (trying on the domestic goddess hat for size) says No honey you have had a hard day, you go put your feet up

M – But you have worked hard too

S – smile… Now in my world I thought that meant he recognised I had worked hard and he would help

Then I realise he has actually sat down to watch TV

Family discussion later as I chuckle at what happened

L (Son, 17) says You should keep it simple and just ask for what you want

Fair Point

I was OK doing the dishes and prepping lunches until I found myself in the kitchen on my own and everyone had disappeared

Sometimes you don't know what you want until you don't have it lol

Q: What do you really want that you have been denying yourself?

"Have the courage to say no.
Have the courage to face the truth.

Do the right thing because it is right.
These are the magic keys to living
your life with integrity."

W Clement Stone

Chapter 8

Influence

"*...the power to have an effect on people or things, or a person or thing that is able to do this... to affect or change how someone or something develops, behaves, or thinks...*"

Cambridge Dictionary

"*Influence is the power to have an important effect on someone or something. If someone influences someone else, they are changing a person or thing in an indirect but important way.*

Sometimes a person who influences another doesn't intend to have any effect, but sometimes they are using influence to benefit themselves. An example of a personal benefit or advantage would be the use of political influence. Influence is also a verb, from Latin – influere to flow in."

Vocabulary.com

How many people would honestly stand up and say that they have never attempted to influence anyone else or that they have never been influenced themselves? Everyone is constantly attempting to exercise influence on a daily basis – probably multiple times a day. Social media is full of opinionated people jumping on their soap boxes at every opportunity to rant about something, hoping desperately that people will agree with them; follow them so they can achieve the albeit fleeting moment of an ego-boosting sense of power and vindication that they are right. The mainstream media has largely transitioned from reporting news (albeit from one perspective or another) to creating it and perhaps even being paid to make it up. It is becoming increasingly difficult to steer a course through it all and not feel influenced.

How do we stand on our own two feet in these circumstances? How can we attempt to get a balanced view based on different perspectives and attempt to stay true to ourselves? There's no easy answer to either of those questions when there are so many people telling us what to think. It does, however, start with awareness and understanding of where you get your information from, to have the best possible chance of exercising free will and the ability to make your own choices amidst the onslaught of 'sponsored propaganda' and fake news. If what is going on in the world is not enough, many others face up to the daily reality of influence and control in the home.

For many, control by narcissistic partners or family members or as a result of bullying in the workplace is an everyday occurrence. Often, this has crept up, escalated over time and quite possibly is accepted as the way things are – or the way that person is. Fear of retribution stops any retaliation. Sometimes the control may be so subtle that it is not even recognised as such and it takes that major event for a person to wake up and understand what has been going on.

When something completely turns your world on its head it is natural that you immediately feel out of control. The rapid follow-up to this is feeling that you no longer have any real influence.

You wake up to the fact that your will has been subverted by another. You may even question your intelligence as you lose your hold on what was normal and your natural state tends towards confusion. This, combined with all the chatter in your head about what has happened, is when you may start to reinforce those beliefs that you are not worthy, or no longer influential because your perception is that no one seems to be listening to you.

When that starts to happen on any level, those are exactly the signals that others will see, regardless of the masks you wear or how you think you are showing up. Others will instinctively pick up on your insecurity and then you will probably hesitate even more, for fear of what they may think. You believe your opinions don't count and stop expressing yourself in the way you want. Before you know it you really have lost your voice and your influence. Suddenly your level of intelligence, your qualifications, or your experience is no longer of any consequence.

People I have worked with explain how they have not felt acknowledged; how they have experienced others interrupting or talking over them, even discounting what they have to say without really listening. I have been told how they have felt that others have perceived them as a person of little or no significance, and in this situation how hard they find it to exert any influence at all. This is when any belief or inner talk, that you are not good enough, will gain a firm foothold as you continue to lose your trust in your own intelligence and capacity to contribute effectively. Sometimes, people start to put themselves down, even to the extent of apologising for their very existence!

As with any self-fulfilling prophecy, the more it happens, the less you are likely to put your own ideas forward and speak up for yourself and so you continue to diminish and lose your power of influence. Sadly, this state of affairs is more than likely to stem from a warped perception, that can rapidly escalate.

Q: How are you sabotaging your own sphere of influence?

Looking back over the time where I now know that I had allowed myself to become invisible, a common thread was that I constantly felt as if I was suffocating. I was closed in by my house and feeling constricted as if the walls were closing in on me – I simply couldn't breathe in there. At work I felt crushed by the people around me as they sapped my energy and spirit until there was no joy left in work that I loved. In relationships I shuttled rapidly from one extreme to the other from breathless, heady in love, to needing air and space from someone trying to be close to me. I couldn't breathe for many reasons and certainly was not inspiring myself or anyone else to any kind of creative or animated feelings. It was a chaotic, confused, and often scary existence with an inconsistency of emotions that was totally exhausting.

Fortunately, I came to understand that in order to be an inspiration to others it was necessary to inspire myself and that began with breathing in and connecting to the heart. When that connection is truly made, there is an awakening, the knowledge that everything comes from within. Once again there is wonder and joy and a sense of what is possible. There comes deep understanding and a sense of self – memories even, of things long forgotten and of course release of things that have been getting in the way. When you are truly in flow, and living your passion, you will stand out as a leader whatever your circumstances or situation. When that happens, those you need will want to follow you and you will influence those in need of what you are here to share.

Key Pattern 6: INFLUENCE

On the other hand, the concept that influence is actually nothing other than the by-product of control came to my attention recently in an online group that I am a member of. This concept is troubling on so many levels and I disagree with the premise entirely. It does, however, seem worthy of further exploration based on my observations of the enthusiastic, unquestioning agreement expressed by others who appear to simply buy into this idea without question.

Those who consider themselves to be controlled, or believe they have been in the past, are the flag wavers at the front of the parade, expending all their energy into condemnation of their perceived torturers. I empathise with their need to reclaim their power; however, I challenge their blind acceptance of this statement as true. Influence in my world is something that everyone has, with the capacity to use it, consciously or unconsciously, for the good or otherwise of themselves and others. Control on the other hand always implies an intentional and often negative agenda, together with manipulation and the subjugation of another for personal or other gain. It is often disguised as for the best, or in the common interest.

We are all born with the capacity to influence and unknowingly exercise this on a daily basis when we share our likes, dislikes, our favourite foods, new clothes, films we love, and so on. We also have the inherent ability to choose for ourselves. The typical cycle of birth to adulthood and beyond unfortunately relieves us of some of our infinite possibility to be whatever and anything we want, as we are coached into acceptable societal, peer group and workplace norms that serve as our reality. We are controlled and educated as to our acceptable influences by those who purport to keep us safe.

Keeping us safe is also a fundamental task of our subconscious; willingly yet somehow unknowingly we relinquish our individual capacity for influence. Teenage rebellions are squashed into conformity until one day we awaken again, understanding there is something else. Control has had dominion over us in the guise of accepted positive influences, of coercion masquerading as love. Both are deliberate acts: one societal consensus, the other the manipulations of one individual over another.

Unfortunately, our subconscious gives permission; relinquishing the power to exert influence that we were gifted at birth by virtue of our own uniqueness. Influence is not the by-product of control, rather control is the misuse of influence. Our every action, every word we speak has the inbuilt capacity to influence others. We all have the choice to shine our light and live in love, or to live in fear and seek to dim the lights of others, through coercion and control. Influence is within us all; we can use or abuse it, steal it or lose it. We are in the midst of a global unravelling of patriarchal control – time to embrace our truth and stand tall. Are you ready to free your influence and be a beacon of light?

Q: How can you free your influence for good?

"Be selective about your external influences.

Your multi-dimensional brain is influenced by everything you see, hear, read, smell, touch, feel or say."

Brian Tracy

Chapter 9

Impact

"...a powerful effect that something, especially something new, has on a situation or person..."

Cambridge Dictionary

"...a physical force (like a collision), an influence (a bad role model or a hero), a forceful consequence or a strong effect..."

Vocabulary.com

A perceived lack of influence is often linked to a perceived lack of impact. The belief that you have no impact (often expressed as "What's the point?") can seriously affect the ability to achieve even the most fundamental of tasks at work or at home. Have you ever found yourself going up the stairs and then wondering why or what you are doing? Do you walk, or more worryingly, drive somewhere and have no recall of how you got there? Have you ever picked something up and then found yourself looking at whatever it is and not knowing what to do with it? These are just a few examples I have come across where the brain fog really takes a hold, and everything becomes a struggle. It's really not you but keeping on top of things becomes difficult, perhaps standards start to slide. You can't seem to get moving and get yourself out of it.

You are on the treadmill of simply existing – waking up, working or not, eating, sleeping and repeat. At least that's how it seems, but what it means is that you simply carry on in the same cycle, whatever that cycle may be. Often you cannot see a way out. Sometimes you may not even see that this is how your life is, because all your senses are dulled, and change does not even feature in your agenda; you are sleepwalking through your life.

This feeling of being insubstantial even dulls the senses. You feel zombie like. Nothing seems to work out the way you intend. You have nothing left to give. You feel like a dull grey shadow of your former self. You no longer feel in charge of your own destiny and finally get to the point where you acknowledge that you are struggling to keep going. I appreciate this may be somewhat similar to how you're feeling. Remember, I've been there myself! Please don't worry… Just keep reading… I promise you, there is light at the end of the tunnel. But just for now ask yourself:

Q: What does your world look like right now?

Potentially, if you are simultaneously reeling from the impact of life-changing events outside of your control, the realisation that you are getting older and that it will never be the same again, then you may well be thinking that you are not important and that your needs are insignificant. Maybe you are simply waking up to the knowledge that you have for many years quite happily relinquished all your personal power to others and now it is time for people to see you differently again.

As a 'slave' to your job, your partner, your children, the real you has been lurking in the shadows, perhaps peeking out occasionally but usually retreating fairly quickly because others do not understand or feel threatened because you do something different. Does anyone else have the memory that sounds something like, "Don't be stupid, you can't do that because…"? Fill in the blanks to suit your own experiences. Is it any wonder that children who are constantly told they are stupid grow up to believe that is true? How many adults are frequently told they are stupid by the significant others in their life?

My personal observations are that it happens far more than we even notice. When we really tune into how people talk to us, or listen to how others speak of or to their colleagues, friends or family, the constant putting down of others is a favourite pastime for some. Social media has spawned the digital 'trolls', who take great pleasure in attacking others seemingly for their own amusement. Is it any wonder that sometimes people choose the easy option to keep their head down, maybe letting others make all the decisions for them and not having to think for themselves?

Part of the process of becoming invisible is the denial or giving up of our birth-given intellect and intelligence, whether knowingly or otherwise. Sometimes it is merely the perception of others that makes this so. As we begin to hand over control of our personal sovereignty, we become slower and at times perhaps even less rational because we have handed over control of our thinking to someone else, by which process we cease to know less and go along with their reasoning and thoughts in contrast to our own that we have now suppressed. It doesn't mean that this capacity is no longer there or is unavailable to us, simply that we are not using it to the full capacity that we are able to and thus we lose our impact.

You do not need to be an extrovert, the life and soul of the party or a proficient public speaker or business leader to create an impact. People it is said do not necessarily remember what you said, or what you did, but they will remember how you made them feel.

We all (pretty much) interact with others on a daily basis under normal circumstances and therefore everything we say and do has the potential to make others feel in a particular way, whether that is what we intended or not. Consequently, all of our interactions deliver our impact.

As we get older and our priorities change, the view that others have of us also changes. Younger generations perceive us as less dynamic and therefore less impactful than their peers. Unfortunately, it would seem that the more we attempt to redress the situation, the worse it actually gets.

An article by Louise Chunn, published in *The Telegraph* on 9 September 2020 and reproduced in the *NZ Herald*, explores why 56 is a tipping point age in women's careers indicating that this issue is not confined to the UK but is actually a global issue. Chunn quotes Lauren Chiren who used to be a senior executive in financial services:

"I had started in this industry in my 30s and became senior quickly. It didn't occur to me there was anything I couldn't do – but the minute I wasn't on my A-game, dynamics changed rapidly, and it unravelled quickly. At the time I thought if I wore sharper suits, or my hair was perfect, with immaculate heels, I could cover up. I worked harder instead of smarter. This is what I see many women go through in their 50s. We've slotted into this very masculine world and left our authentic selves at home."

My first thought on reading this was – exactly! This so totally reflects my own experience and that of many other women who have shared their stories with me. Chunn, goes on to say:

"Women of 50-plus may be the fastest growing economically active group in the UK but who says they want to engage with work in the same way they did when they were starting out? Especially in the COVID period, when many of us are rethinking our working lives altogether right now."

I would go so far as to suggest that many of us are not just rethinking our working lives; we are rethinking our entire lives. We have arrived at a stage where the opinions and influence of others matters less and less. We know we have strengths that we have kept from the world as we have donned our different masks and juggled conflicting priorities in order to be all things to all people and very little to ourselves. No wonder there comes a point where it seems we have lost our impact.

If we can rise above the inclination to not be bothered, then we have our intelligence and our experience to provide a solid framework for whatever we decide to do next. Chunn suggests that 56 is the tipping point because this is now an age beyond being in your early 50s with 60 rapidly approaching. For many women, actually, the struggle between feeling washed up and/or set on a new path will resonate with anyone feeling at all dissatisfied or demoralised about their career. As that voice in your head whispers: if not now, when?

Whether a significant event prompts a rethink or just a dawning realisation that things could be different, it is apparent that women the world over are not settling quietly into 'grannyhood' as they move beyond their mid-50s. Instead, they are dusting themselves off, reinventing who they are and preparing to embrace their third age, the so-called 'golden age' of adulthood with gusto.

For me personally, the years between 56 and 60 have been the years of getting everything in place to finally move into the next phase of living my dream. One month shy of 60, I made it to Italy (during a fortuitous break in COVID-related restrictions) and here I am now, finally between the lake and the mountains, setting the stage to make an impact in the world that deep down I always knew was my true destiny.

Key Pattern 7: IMPACT

"The only limit to your impact is your imagination and commitment."

Tony Robbins

Chapter 10

Imagination

"...the ability to form pictures in the mind... something that you think exists or is true, although in fact it is not real or true... the ability to think of new ideas..."

Cambridge Dictionary

"...the process of forming images or concepts in the mind, often images of things that are not really there. That shark in your bathtub must have been in your imagination – or was it?

Often shunned for living in a dream world, imagination is behind unicorns, Big Foot, and excessive daydreaming. But it's humans' ability to picture what is not there, and to be resourceful and creative, that is behind many of our achievements. Maybe that's why Albert Einstein said, 'Imagination is more important than knowledge.' After all, without a little imagination, we wouldn't have the pyramids, the space shuttles, or the Star Wars trilogy."

Vocabulary.com

Let's now talk about your imagination, which in some ways is a bit of a conundrum when taken in the context of who you are and whether you are fully visible as your true self or not. Whether you are keeping it real or living in a fantasy of your own creation. On the one hand, your imagination is in overdrive and is furnishing you with all sorts of scenarios that do very little to move you forward and a great deal to drag you back and keep you in the past. On the other hand, your ability to use your imagination for anything constructive is probably at an all-time low and it is quite likely that you are telling yourself you can't think straight. To some degree you may have lost touch with reality as your imagination is stuck on repeat, constantly replaying the scenes from the past, wondering how you could have done things differently.

Then you jump to your current situation and cannot imagine how you can change things for the better. Your negative thoughts take up all the space, focusing on the past, things you cannot change. Consequently, there's no room for you to imagine the future and therefore create anything new or different. You are stuck in a rut and you are unable to find a way out.

You probably talk yourself out of any ideas you may have, or you allow other people to put you off. Maybe you don't even realise that you are in this rut, stuck on the hamster wheel going round and round in circles, because now this is all you know and this small space has become your world – your life. Anger probably lives here, as do any other negative emotions you continually visit. They serve little purpose other than to steal your energy – and your time. Ultimately you stay stuck in a place where your energy is so depleted that you barely recognise yourself.

The good news about energy is that it infinite. Every individual has the inherent capacity to raise their vibration, which in turn increases their energy, thereby enabling them to create new pathways that lead to the change they want.

Q: In what ways would you like to reshape your future?

When your ideas are no longer your own (even if you think they are), your imagination is almost non-existent – on some level you are simply existing. There is no room for innovation, anything new in your life, no change even if deep down you desire change. You have probably become stuck in a rut and you are unable to find a way to make things different, any ideas, big or small, and you may feel you have nothing to contribute.

Even if you are involved in idea generation or innovation in your place of work, it seems that all your ideas are overlooked, or no one hears you. Maybe your ideas are ridiculed and so you withdraw further and become less enthusiastic and inclined to engage. Maybe you don't even realise that you are in this rut, stuck on the hamster wheel going round and round in circles because now this is all you know and everything else has been suppressed. This has become your life and your light is no longer shining. You are no longer shining, expressing yourself and who you are.

Your imagination is yours alone and is one aspect of you that sets you apart from everyone else. Good or bad, happy or sad, whatever you imagine defines your life. In fact, what you imagine creates your life. Past experiences somehow become even harder or even better when we are in constant reflection through either the mists of anger or rose-tinted spectacles. Our brain, our memories, simply become reinforced and further embedded. Memories expand and take up all the space. Unfortunately, from here we can only create a future out of what we already know, what we focus on. So, 'Smile and the world smiles with you'. It's hard not to return a smile after all. Also, 'Misery loves company'. When you become stuck there, you have a message on repeat, your focus, so that's what you get more of and you may well be surrounded by like-minded people!

Key Pattern 8: IMAGINATION

Obviously, we are not all destined to change the world. We are not all inventors of life-changing, ground-breaking products, but each and every day we all have the power of choice – the power to choose to be an innovator in our own life. You too have the power to make changes, to do something new, to start something for the first time. Every minute of every day (each and every one of them) you are making your own choice. The path you create is the route of your unique innovative life or a life that you have allowed someone else to lead you down.

We all have the choice to go along with the wishes of those around us, maybe to fit in, to be the same as, to not stand out, to live as we are expected to live. These are largely to do with the foundations of society and looking back through history we can see that the Greeks, Romans, Egyptians and other civilisations all had their societal rules and ways of behaving or conforming, just as we do today. I am not suggesting that you need to go out and break all the rules of society in order to live your own innovative life; there are more than enough criminals and the like out there already. I simply suggest that you ask yourself a few questions about your life.

- What is your purpose?

- What are you here for?

- How do you interact with others?

- How do you behave in different situations?

- Do you live in the present? Or do you constantly look back to the past and things you cannot change? Maybe you yearn for the future that will happen when things are different.

- Are you mindful? Do you understand the consequences of your thoughts and actions?

- Are you happy with different aspects of your life? (truly happy with your finances, your family, relationships, health and so on).

Take a little time to think about these questions and see what comes into your mind and awareness. Remember you can't tackle everything at once and you too can experience the cumulative effect of many small changes. Small changes can have a profound effect on your life and the outcomes you achieve.

Easy to say perhaps but how do you go about it? How do you become an innovator and introduce new things into your own life? Obvious as it may be, the first thing is that you have to see the problem and then you have to want to do something about it. When you look deeper and see what the causes are, then you will know what to change. Where to start? Innovation is a broad topic in any context, so let's consider other aspects to this subject that also have a significant impact and influence on our personal journey.

The Carney Intuitive Imagination Process

I have created a model that is as applicable to a life process as a business process. The specific areas that I consider relevant here are all aligned with our intuition. We start by placing our imagination at the centre, from where it directly impacts all of the other four areas in this model, and highlight that innovation is simply a connecting part of the process together with ideas, improvement and implementation. If you are able to tune into and listen to your intuition, that tells you what you need to do (or not to do), then you will be able to use your wonderful imagination to develop and bring to fruition the innovative ideas that will deliver improvements to whatever aspect of your life you want to work on. Once you know what you are going to do then of course you can implement whatever ideas you have come up with.

Normally we are conditioned to believing that ideas are always innovative, however that doesn't have to be the case. Actually, in all probability they are not entirely new. We humans have a great and documented history of repeating our history. It might be fairer to say "new for now." Maybe what we are actually experiencing is not something entirely new but the rediscovery of something that came before. The Romans had a toilet system long before Thomas Crapper developed his flushing toilet. Leonardo da Vinci was a man well ahead of his time and engineers who have built from his designs have found that they do actually work.

The more I study and the further I explore on my spiritual and life journey, the more I conclude that everything is already within us – stored, forgotten perhaps, until someone discovers or invents something new to create something different and newly relevant for our time. We call it innovation but maybe our innovations occur when we tune into our inner consciousness and find things that were previously lost. Maybe we finally see the person we were meant to be and begin the process to reintroduce that person to the world. That process begins with imagination.

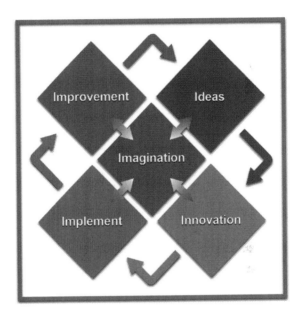

The Carney Intuitive Imagination Process Model

1. Imagination

Let's look more deeply into the imagination. You will more than likely have heard the saying 'If you believe it you can achieve it'. I have no intention of going into detail here about The Law of Attraction, manifesting abundance or the like, as there are plenty of books, videos and webinars that explore this subject. Suffice to say I am a believer and have more than enough examples to verify my belief that our thoughts create our reality. Each one of us is born with the power of imagination and this is truly a huge power; there is no one that has no imagination and you should not underestimate how this works.

Whatever you imagine your life to be is exactly what it will be. Your mind and the universe will work in unison to give you exactly what you create with your thoughts even if you don't think you are outwardly using your imagination.

To illustrate this a little more clearly, who do you know who say things like:

- "I get the flu every Christmas/winter"

- "My job is so boring"

- "I will never... be able to..."

- "I have no money/I can't afford..."?

Perhaps you say or think such things yourself. Guess what? All of those statements are things imagined before any reality kicks in. It is exactly what you imagine and therefore *exactly* what you are requesting and more than likely exactly what you get – flu every Christmas, a boring job that never gets any more interesting. You get the picture. Expand this concept to all areas of your life and consider where your imagination has created a situation that you do not want, where your imagination has granted you invisibility.

Do you tell yourself (or allow others to tell you) that you are no good, useless, pathetic, stupid, silly, worthless, ignorant, weak or any number of other put-downs? Do you now find yourself exactly that? Funny how it works – maybe you start off challenging such labels, then you question whether or not there is something wrong with you and whether it is true until eventually you 'know' it is and you have imagined it into reality.

The more you start to take back control and use your imagination to create a different reality, the easier it will become to make changes. Start small with little changes and as you begin to achieve what you have imagined then you will gather momentum, have more ideas and get everything flowing positively in the way you want. You need to make a conscious decision to take control, to know that you are enough, that you are worthy and make sure that you guard your thoughts (your imagination) because it is very easy to put the wrong spin on things and still not get what you want.

The key here is NOT to focus on having less of what you don't want: debt, weight, love and the like. If you say things like; "I want to get rid of my debts," "I want to lose weight," then you are still focused on exactly what you don't want, and because this is where your imagination goes, together with the fear of not paying the bills, not fitting into a particular outfit, then you are more likely to get more debt and put on more weight. Turn it around for example to, "I have plenty of money in my bank account," or "I am my ideal weight" and your imagination will be triggered in a completely different way. It is important to remember that this takes practice and does not happen overnight. Do not give up, be consistent and remember that the cumulative effect of lots of little changes can be enormous. Don't dismiss little things, follow your instinct, and use your imagination to develop the life-changing ideas to create the improvements that you are looking for.

Q: Is your imagination being innovative and creative or negative and destructive?

2. Ideas

Ideas – what are they and does everyone have them? Yes of course everyone has ideas. It makes me mad when I hear people say, "I am not an ideas person." They could be, they just choose not to be. OK, so some of us have more creative, business, or maybe world-changing ideas than others but we all have ideas. Are you the quiet person at the back who doesn't tell anyone your idea for fear of being ridiculed or not listened to? Do you always apply your filters at home and at work because you don't believe in yourself? Are you the person who mutters at the coffee machine, "I told them it (fill in the blanks)"? Do you allow others to always take control so your own ideas are suppressed?

There is always more than one way and the answers are already inside you. If you allow your ideas, your visioning creativity, to expand through your energy and flow, then nothing or no one can stop you from achieving whatever it is you really want. Don't worry if you can't work out how to make these ideas a reality. That comes later. One of the best ways to find out ideas to improve a process is always to ask the person doing the job. They are usually the last to be consulted but they probably have the most useful, simple and effective ideas that will often make life easier for all concerned. One of the classic examples that I always use in training is the story of 'the empty soapbox'.

This actually happened in one of Japan's big cosmetics companies, when a consumer complained they had bought a soap box that was empty. The problem was immediately isolated to the assembly line, which transported all the packaged boxes of soap to the delivery department. Engineers were put to work to solve the problem and came up with an expensive X-ray machine that required two people to watch the high-resolution monitors checking all the soap boxes as they progressed down the line to ensure they were not empty.

A factory operative when tasked with solving the same problem simply purchased a strong electric fan which he pointed at the assembly line. When the soap boxes passed the fan, any empty boxes were simply blown off the line. The moral of the story is to always look for the simplest possible solutions to solve the problem. When you train yourself to focus on solutions not on problems you will get far better results. Similarly, if you only look at what you do not have in your life you will find you don't have anything; however, if you look at what you do have you will discover that you have everything. It is all within you.

So that's your job – you are the person in charge of the process of your life. You know better than anyone else what needs to change. You probably already have some pretty good ideas of what could work to get the results you want – the job, the relationships, the finances, the health, the leisure time, social life – any of it or all of it. Now is the time to just make a few notes of what you would like to change.

Q: What ideas do you already have that could change your life for the better?

3. Innovation

For the last few years, innovation has been a buzzword in many large organisations. When they decided that they were standing still, they needed to innovate in order to make change happen. I have been personally involved in a number of innovation programmes and the objectives are always, to find ways to do things differently, to move forward. Essentially, these schemes are an organised step up from the staff suggestion boxes of old. The point is to empower staff to think freely and come up with great ideas to change the way a company does things.

It is clear, however, that there is often greater management interest in cost-saving suggestions that deliver immediate benefits rather than initiatives that required effort, investment and a longer wait for the realisation of benefits. Needless to say, there is always great anticipation that a massive game-changing idea will surface that will truly change an organisation. Unfortunately, these ideas are few and far between and innovation schemes are simply about idea generation, to see if new methods or ways of doing the same things can be found. One hopes that if new ideas do surface they are put in front of the right people with the vision and understanding to propel them into reality.

Success or failure rests with the management teams that are able to give life to these new ideas by authorising the go-ahead and any necessary funding or resource required. What is often missed is that innovation is not just about the big ideas. What is frequently overlooked is the cumulative effect of multiple small ideas and how this can also result in huge impact. My favourite illustration of this concept is about the Winnebago Company, the famous recreational vehicle manufacturer in the United States. Here's what happened:

In the early 1990s Winnebago experienced high demand for a particular model including a high demand for optional extras that brought the model to its vehicle weight limit. The chairman John K Hanson asked all staff for ideas to reduce the weight of the vehicle. He very quickly received over 200 ideas, including: removing hooks from the chassis that were only used during shipping of the chassis; not installing carpet under beds that were bolted flush to the floor; and removing special brackets originally used to hold mirrors no longer used. Some of the ideas saved just a couple of ounces but the cumulative effect was to enable the saving that enabled Winnebago to add the extras and keep below the weight limit for the vehicle. Plus, it was all staff not just the 'expert' engineers who got involved in the process.

By now you may be thinking OK I get that but what has it got to do with me? What does innovation have to do with personal power, being real and revealing your true self? Let's consider some innovators. Sometimes it may just be that **you** do bring the next big thing to the world and this is what sets you apart from the rest. Consider Mark Zuckerberg, Steve Jobs, Freddie Laker – all innovators. Looking further back in history, we find Thomas Edison and Alexander Graham Bell without whom the world as we know it would not be the same. When these innovators came to the fore, one thing they have in common is they challenged the status quo and often caused upheaval, giving the world or existing industry a wake-up call that necessitated a strategic rethink.

Enter low-cost airlines, personal computers, and virtual friends! Those innovators that prevailed never gave up, they were true to themselves and they refused to be swayed by those who didn't believe in them or what they were doing. Great inventors and their innovations change the world, small incremental changes can collectively make a huge difference. When it comes to your world the choice is yours entirely. The 'Go big or go home' slogan that originated in the 90s does not apply. The first step is simply to understand the power of your imagination and what is going on at the moment.

4. Implement

The thing about having new, innovative life-changing ideas is that you have to implement them, or nothing will change. It's the same in a business context. There's a lot of talk sometimes, and not very much action. Have you ever been 'consulted' in a work environment, perhaps asked for your ideas? Months go by and nothing actually happens. Have you been involved in a project which has been given the green light to go ahead, only to falter because the project team also have day jobs and can't be released to do project work? After a while, projects get binned or put on the back burner because they are no longer priority or perhaps no longer relevant at all.

It's a painful experience, all the excitement and enthusiasm at the beginning gradually gets crushed. Often this happens because suddenly 'everything' is a project. There ends up being far too many, with too little resource to go around and not enough time or money to implement them. Add to the mix the fact that far too many projects are kicked off with no real thought to company strategy. If they don't tie in with the strategy, then why are they being started? It is hardly any wonder that people get demoralised and lose motivation.

There are, however, key practices to ensure successful implementation, and where organisations have a good project management framework they can and do achieve great success. The parallel to implementing the new ideas and the changes in your life is to have a good strategy to align with and some structured processes to keep you on track. It sounds really simple doesn't it? But so many people don't seem to be able to get off the starting blocks. The next thing is they are complaining again that they never get anywhere, nothing they do ever works and...

I'm sure you get the picture, perhaps you have even strayed there yourself. The good news is there is a solution. It involves a plan and it involves a process to put that plan into effect. It also requires commitment, accountability and the understanding of what to do when the plan slips, which inevitably it will.

5. Improvement

As you know, since I left the corporate world I have been on a journey to get my visibility back, to rediscover who I really am and to take charge once and for all of my life. Improvement in so many areas of my life has been a key activity in this process. I am grateful for the things that I did learn and some of the wonderful experiences that I was privileged to enjoy on my corporate journey (it wasn't all bad!). I view it now as a necessary part of my improvement. If it hadn't happened I would not be where I am today. At times it feels like it has been a long road, but then again, the thing about improvement is that it never ends. As long as we keep breathing there is always something we can learn, something new that will help us change the way we view the world, or something that will change our world.

In the Quality Standards world that I have inhabited for many years the term is 'continuous improvement'. This means that once you have implemented some successful changes you don't just sit on your backside and assume that it's done and all will be well forever. You really do need to keep a handle on things and monitor what is going on in order to react quickly if things slide, or your results are not as expected. Daily practices help to reinforce and embed change.

"To be yourself in a world that is constantly trying to make you something else is the greatest accomplishment."

Ralph Waldo Emerson

Chapter 11

Independence

"...the ability to live your life without being helped or influenced by other people..."

To be independent is to be:

"...not influenced or controlled in any way by other people, events, or things."

Cambridge Dictionary

"...the state of being free of the control of some other person, country or entity. Revolutions are all about obtaining independence.

Independence comes from a nice medieval French word, depenre, meaning 'to hang from' or 'to hang down'. The 'in' at the beginning is Latin for 'not', so the word originally meant 'not hanging from...'"

Vocabulary.com

When life has eroded your visibility and sense of self, your independence once valued is barely recognisable – you question who you are and what you are here for. We have already highlighted that you are not firing on all cylinders. You've probably ceased to function on every level. Maybe you think you're doing OK, but in reality, you no longer know who you are any more. Regardless of what life-changing event has devastated your world, you remain many things to many people – but who are you to yourself? Even if you have not experienced a catastrophe that has plunged you into chaos, you can probably begin to evaluate your own situation and assess the signs that you may not be as independent as you thought, you are in fact literally hanging from someone else.

Being unable to make even simple decisions without referring back to someone else, usually a significant other, is an obvious sign that you may be losing the ability to think for yourself and allowing yourself to be controlled in some way. I'm talking here about successful people who earn (their own) good money that are incapable of buying often trivial inexpensive things that they want because they have to 'check first' or the other person 'might not like it'. At this point, I am not suggesting that people should not check in with their significant other when it matters and of course when something is important. There are many healthy relationships where regular 'consulting,' with the other half is not cause for alarm. There is, however, a fine line where natural politeness and consideration for another spills over and becomes something else. It's at that point that someone subjugates themselves to another to such a degree they become unhealthily dependent.

You are, or have been, son or daughter, husband, wife, partner, mother, father, grandparent, worker, colleague, manager, carer and more. Most likely, you have spent much of your life juggling all of the commitments you have to all of these people in your life. As much as they depend on you, or have depended on you in the past, when something changes, it's like waking up, but at the same time feeling like a deer caught in the car headlights. Clients have told me that they have reached a stage where they believe who they are is of little or no significance because they no longer know how to assert their own independence. It comes as a huge shock when they are forced to do so.

Similar feelings can be triggered as the result of a job loss. Senior and very successful people who have given everything to an organisation for many years, feeling like they are part of a work family, are suddenly cast aside when 'new blood' arrives and makes sweeping changes. The chess pieces move and a person is no longer in the game – a game that previously they were the master of. It's a huge shock that triggers many emotions: frustration, anger, perhaps even sadness, depression and often shame.

Shame that comes from loss of position, a changed status and the absolute killer; the inability to speak up or speak out about it as the settlement is based on the agreement to be silent, or to pretend it's actually redundancy or early retirement. There's always a spin to protect the company when they hang their loyal people out to dry. The world turns and everything carries on as before except you are no longer involved and are left attempting to pick up the pieces of your broken life. Unwanted independence can feel like a lonely place, but independence that is embraced can also be where freedom lies.

Key Pattern 9: INDEPENDENCE

After possibly a lifetime of co-dependence in the purest sense of being needed and believing your own needs will be met, it is hard when that connection is suddenly gone. The same is true whether it involves a relationship, family, friends or work. How do you deal with this new independence when the very concept is completely alien to you? It is often an exhausting scenario but it's still not the whole story. There is another huge sign that you are probably missing and we will look at that in the next chapter, but for now:

Q: What does independence mean to you?

Independence, in my opinion, is so much more than being able to take care of yourself, or to not have to rely on anyone else for any kind of support – financial or otherwise. When we take a closer look at independence, we notice that we spend our formative years becoming independent. As we learn to walk and talk, to do things for ourselves, whether it is choosing our own clothes, getting dressed, tying our own shoelaces, getting breakfast, or walking to school we are applauded for each milestone we achieve. Then somewhere, somehow as we reach our pinnacle of independence, we start to lose it again. I don't mean suddenly not being able to get dressed or walk or talk. (I also recognise, that certain medical conditions or accidents may rob some of their independence and they may need to be dependent on others as a result. This is not, however, what I am talking about here.)

As we 'escape' the controls of our childhood, peer group membership demands a certain lack of individuality replacing it with conformity to the group ideals. As we move on from the authority and control of our parents, we often cede authority and control to our peer group. The way we speak, act and dress may all be 'controlled' by the act of belonging to a particular group. Naturally there is a huge variety in levels of immersion in a particular subculture and at the extreme level there is no independence outside of the group whatsoever. Here, I am thinking of cult societies such as Jonestown founded by Jim Jones in Guyana, where a total of 918 people were found dead, most of whom were persuaded under duress to commit mass suicide in 1978.

I struggle to understand how a need to belong, to be the same as others, can lead people to give up control of every single aspect of their own independence including their right to live. What is clear is that however such situations arise, it becomes almost impossible for a person that has given over so much of themselves to get out, and perhaps as in this case to get out alive. My belief is that in such cults people are controlled in every aspect of what they believe, they depend on the leader and the group for both opinion and livelihood and become obliged to that leader for their very existence. The validity of that existence comes from the membership itself and taking part in all the associated activities. The group takes over, there is no longer a true sense of any individuality or independence from the group. There is in fact no room for independence as the group mentality prevails.

A famous fictional example of this is William Golding's *Lord of the Flies*. Here the various themes include the conflict between individuality and the power of the group to sway individuality that results in significant crossed boundaries of rational and emotional reactions. The struggle between right and wrong, moral and immoral is played out in the interactions between leaders and followers, rapidly degenerating from civilisation to savagery as fears are realised and exploited. How our perceptions of strength or weakness can be used to manipulate others in order to control both thoughts and behaviour is brilliantly imagined, and yet, the imagination and the telling of a tale are but a whisper away from reality.

The loss or gain of independence is an experience that most people will consciously experience at various stages of life. Often life will complete a full circle from the dependency of the new-born baby on its parents to the reliance of the dying elderly on their own children or carers. This clearly is physical dependence but there is so much more that happens in between these beginning and end of life stages that may have a far more significant emotional impact on how someone's life plays out. Inner strength or weakness in particular situations can make all the difference to the eventual outcome.

Peer group membership as already mentioned is often a 'rite of passage' club, so what if we look more closely at some widely identifiable sub-cultural groups such as hippies, Hells Angels, street gangs, and not to be accused of any sort of bias here, what about yuppies, nerds, sloanes, preppies and more? What happens when you think about each of these groups? Do you instantly picture a particular type of look – clothing and associated accessories? Do you imagine places where these 'tribes' can be found? Does your mind present you with images of expected behaviour? Do you see yourself belonging to a particular set of people where you dress and act according to what you believe is appropriate in this environment?

Your initial reaction may well be no of course not, however look a little closer. This is not just about the extreme stereotypes. Everywhere I look I see people dressing and behaving in order to 'fit in'.

- Many teenage boys are still wearing their trousers at half-mast insisting on showing off their underwear and walking around looking like they just pooped in their nappy.

- Teenage girls (and some older ones too) seem to have a penchant for orange fake tan, enormous fake eyelashes, pencilled brows, vertiginous heels and too tight mini-dresses that leave nothing to the imagination.

- Plenty of middle-aged men regularly sport football shirts as their casual attire of choice, although the majority would be hard pressed to run around on the pitch for any length of time.

- Yet another subset of middle-aged and older men are spending weekends and evenings cycling around the countryside in sweaty lycra as they pedal in large groups elephant-style – nose to tail, nose to tail.

All of these lifestyle choices by nature of their adoption clearly indicate a reliance on the herd mentality to validate the chosen look. Initially a radical look may be chosen to demonstrate independence from one group, perhaps family or culture, (think mods, rockers, punks, hippies). The end result indicates at least some level of dependence on another group. The individual feels visible because they are an accepted part of their chosen club. From an outsider's perspective there is no individuality or independence to be seen – they all look the same to me. How often do we hear this statement about different groups of people, whether they are youth groups or cultural variations in looks and conventions?

There is a certain incongruity to joining a tribe in order to express yourself, only to become so immersed that only the whole tribe can be seen as it subsumes the individuals to its signature look and feel. Does collective visibility therefore negate individual visibility? Is it more important to belong and identify with a specific group or groups than to stand out on one's own and be unique? Does anyone else think it's strange that even when we don't have to wear a uniform we find countless ways of creating them? Is it only possible to see any individuality once inside the group?

What level of independence do group members have? What happens when someone leaves a group? Are we programmed during our early years to surrender independence on a variety of levels as we mix with our peers, form relationships and perhaps get married? There are some examples of what appears to be voluntary surrender of independence and many more where it comes as the result of a controlling other. I wonder whether anyone understands what they have given up until they struggle to find a way out.

Adults who escape an abusive, controlling relationship for example may finally be able to achieve independence and freedom to be who they are meant to be. Often this can be a long hard struggle on many fronts. Sadly, we do not have to look too far from our own circle to find someone that has. Brenda Dempsey, a woman

I am proud to call my friend, is an amazing example of someone who managed to break free from the abuse, to fight and win her freedom. After suffering years of psychological and verbal abuse Brenda finally broke free, becoming homeless before she found a safe house where she and her four young children could feel secure.

At the time Brenda was also managing to juggle daily support for her ailing parents and studying in the final year of her teaching degree. She never lost sight of the fact that this degree was her ticket to freedom and despite many challenges along the way completed it, and as a teacher was finally able to provide her children with a different kind of life. After retiring from teaching, Brenda began to tell her story, realising the cathartic power of being able to do this. In 2019 she brought together a group of 33 women who were finally able to tell their own stories. The result was *Voices of Courage*, an anthology of inspirational true stories – of pivotal moments where women took back control of their lives and regained their independence. I am honoured to have been selected as one of those contributing authors.

From its core, the story I shared has evolved further, remaining at the heart of this book. Finally, I actually feel independent enough to complete it. Meanwhile Brenda continues to work tirelessly, encouraging others to find their voice and allow their story to be told. Having managed to dramatically transform her own life through sheer grit and determination, Brenda knows exactly what it takes.

My personal research would suggest that the key to regaining independence is to take back control of our thoughts. Once we wake up and understand that the major part of how we think has been defined by the collective or a significant other, only then can we regain our own opinions and independence.

"To find yourself, think for yourself."

Socrates

Chapter 12

Intuition

"...an ability to understand or know something without needing to think about it or use reason to discover it, or a feeling that shows this ability..."

Cambridge Dictionary

"...Instinctive knowing (without the use of rational processes... quick understanding to interpret but without using reasoning or perception, a snap judgment... from the Latin roots in meaning 'at' or 'on' and tueri meaning 'look at, watch over'. If we use our intuition it means that we don't always make the correct interpretation... the Australian writer Christina Stead wrote 'Intuition is not infallible; it only seems to be the truth'."

Vocabulary.com

The difference between Instinct and Intuition

It is important to clarify the differences between instinct and intuition, because it has become apparent especially during my research and the writing of this book that many people use the terms interchangeably. Although the definitions refer to instinctive knowing, they are talking about the way in which intuition makes itself known to us rather than an involuntary response where we react without conscious thought.

To expand on the dictionary definitions above, there is a clear distinction and instinct is defined as follows:

"...the way people or animals naturally react or behave, without having to think or learn about it..."

Cambridge Dictionary

Instinct then is an innate pattern of behaviour when one acts without conscious intention. It's an unconscious skill that is triggered perhaps when we face danger, the flight or fight mode that is an instant reaction when faced with a charging animal or perhaps an impending punch. We run, we duck, we don't even have to think about it. Intuition on the other hand would be more around the feeling of something. A sense in your gut perhaps that there is danger lurking. You can't see the dangerous animal yet but somehow you know there's one close by. You don't have to think about it but you simply know because you feel it in your body.

I believe this is worth exploring in the context of how what we do or don't do in any given situation is fundamentally significant to our level of visibility or shade of invisibility in our current life situation, or the memory of events previously experienced. Our instincts tend to remain intact and will generally continue to function, unless we are perhaps under the influence of alcohol or drugs. Intuition, however, seems to be there all the time but we can ignore it, switch it off somehow and therefore exercise free will over whether we use it or not.

How often do you have an intuition about something? When you know the right course of action, or that you are in the right place, or that a person is the one you are meant to be with? Alternatively, do you allow it to kick in only when something or someone is not right; you don't feel safe, perhaps even sense danger?

Do you always act on your intuition, or do you often ignore it? How often do you *allow* someone else to talk you into something that you know is wrong, not what you want to do, not in your best interests or is something you know you should not be doing? Do you find yourself being talked out of doing what you want to do (even when your intuition is screaming NO!)?

I bet you can think of some very real examples where you did not go with your own intuition – the question is why? I can probably give hundreds of examples to illustrate this and I am sure you can too. Here are just a couple to get you thinking.

I chose a module in the final year of my degree that I knew I wasn't really interested in instead of a module I wanted to take because someone else persuaded me that 'I would love it'. Well I didn't, but honestly, what was I thinking? Why did I not have the confidence to stand up for myself, to go with what I really wanted, to follow my intuition and do a course that I was much better suited to rather than be persuaded by someone that this option was a good fit for me when this person clearly had different criteria from me?

How about work? Have you taken a job that you knew wasn't right for you? Did you get stressed, hate every minute of it, dread going to work, get sick even? We are taught at school all about getting our grades and then going off to work. Careers guidance (in my experience) is often fairly random and can be based on what subjects we are studying rather than what interests us – at least that was my impression. The suggestions given to me were banking or insurance and funnily enough I have worked in both. I got out of banking after a couple of years but spent nearly a decade in insurance – most of it wondering what on earth I was doing there.

Fast-forward a good few years and some extensive (paid for) careers evaluation for my son and the conclusion was that he would make a good actuary. Maybe so, but he is much happier being himself as a musician – he loves it and thankfully people love him and his music. You spend a lot of time at work, earning a living to pay your bills, so why not do something you love and love what you do?

What does your intuition tell you about what you really want to do? If you ask yourself and listen carefully, you will hear your inner truth speaking to you. Whatever aspect of your life you are considering, whatever decision or choice you are deliberating, if you learn to *trust* your intuition. Everyone has the skill of intuitive insight; the challenge now is to learn how to use it effectively. Tuning into and tuning up your intuition can help you make decisions that will lead to making the changes that will set you on your true path. You don't have to go out and buy anything, you already have it, and when you start to use it you will simply just *know* the right thing to do.

Key Pattern 10: INTUITION

When we are talking about danger, perhaps instinct does kick in when our fight or flight mode is triggered, but what about ordinary day-to-day situations? If instinct is an involuntary reaction to something that causes a certain reaction, is it possible to subdue our natural instincts? Is instinct at times simply a layer of our intuition that it is also possible to suppress, for example when suffering abuse of any kind? Instinct should cause you to fight back in order to protect yourself and maybe this is what happened to start with. With repetition that option may simply make things worse as the natural instinct to fight back may actually cause more harm in such circumstances. Do your instincts cause you to react or have your circumstances led you to suppress them even in the face of harm? Perhaps that's when you do listen to your intuition as it steps up to protect you.

Often though, there is a big red flag constantly waving under your nose and it is more than likely you won't be able to see it, even if someone points it out to you! Your intuition – always with you and often jumping up and down to attract your attention, but sadly completely ignored.

So, what does it look like when you don't follow your intuition? You probably become unsure of yourself and your own intentions because you no longer trust or even hear your intuition. Possibly, you no longer know why you do certain things or perhaps why you do anything. Sometimes you may even fear that your intuition is proved right because this may put you under a spotlight where you don't want to be right now. So, knowingly or unknowingly now, you hide. You may hide with the best of intention, at least in your own mind; it feels right but if your intention is to hide, to not speak your truth, to not stand up for what you believe, then your intention ultimately diverts you from the path of your true purpose and why you are here. You and your true self are now invisible to others and also to yourself. The worst of it is nobody knows, not even you. It is what you have become but it is not you – not your essence, not your soul, not your light, not who you were meant to be.

When you shut your intuition down, you don't hear it, feel it, sense it in any way. You have probably not been picking up signals from those around you or taking note of what you see for some time. It is likely you have not been paying attention even when your intuition has been screaming at you that something is not right. The conditioning of your situation means you no longer heed what it tells you, you dismiss its messages, perhaps because to listen and act accordingly would make you stand out or force you to stand up for yourself.

Q: What is your intuition telling you that you're not listening to?

The voice in your head is not your crazy mind, it is not crazy at all. The voice in your head is your barometer, your guidance and support. The more you listen to your intuition, then you will discover how you know the answers and then you will begin to trust that information, and more importantly you will begin to trust and believe in yourself.

"You must train your intuition —
you must trust the small voice inside
you which tells you exactly
what to say, what to decide."

Ingrid Bergman

Chapter 13

Case Studies

The Good Girl – always holding back

A friend of mine called me one day and simply said, "Let's do it." She had known about my book from its inception, had participated in some research and initial exploration around some of the themes and declared that she often felt invisible. She was now ready to become fully visible and wanted to come and work with me to explore what lay beneath this – both the emotion and ongoing behaviour plus repeated patterns that kept her invisible. Immediately we established that on a scale of 0 to 10, with 0 feeling totally invisible and 10 being fully visible, she was currently at a 5 and at times had felt much lower. So how to get her to be a 10?

Very quickly we established that her patterns of hiding stemmed from events in her childhood and this had resulted in lifelong behaviour patterns of always stepping back, hiding what she really wanted to do or say, keeping the peace and always looking after everyone around her – including perhaps those who should have been looking after her. In addition, she highlighted ongoing insecurities about not being good enough or even independent enough at times to do what she really wanted to do. We then reviewed all the aspects that I have identified as those things that we give up or suppress as we become invisible.

It became clear that to some degree she was able to identify with each of these areas as aspects of her true self that she had either consciously or unconsciously suppressed. This was partly a response to the behaviour of those around her that instilled a fundamental need to always be the well-behaved good girl and not rock the boat or draw attention to herself in any way. Unfortunately, at school additional insecurities were manifested as a result of her perception that other pupils were treated as 'teachers' pets' and held up as being cleverer than her.

Perception is reality – right? In this case that reality became firmly fixed in the mind of a young girl to develop limiting beliefs: that she wasn't clever enough, that she couldn't do things as well as others, that she was insignificant and more. The lack of independence coupled with the belief that she wasn't clever enough stopped her from going to university. Later, ignoring her own intuition and not being true to her inner integrity, and putting other people's needs before her own, were key factors that stopped her from taking up a dream job overseas – a decision that to this day she still regrets.

Fast-forward and this lady is a businesswoman who does however feel that she has not reached the level of success she is aiming for and we began to explore what was at the bottom of this. As we went deeper it became apparent that the insecurities from childhood were still influencing current behaviour which manifested as a direct response to specific situations. Those situations turned out to be where rejection was perceived and that rejection was immediately internalised and taken personally.

The subsequent behaviour was to replay the old patterns of not being good enough and to tell herself that people didn't want to hear what she had to say – who was she anyway? This in turn resulted in a withdrawal from the type of activity that would lead towards the achievement of her goals. It was always one step forward, two steps back. The negative response of one person immediately negating the positive responses of many others.

The outcome, I am delighted to say, is that she now has far more confidence, does not hold back in the same way and has even been on a speaker panel at a national conference.

Walking on eggshells

How many times have you heard or used the expression 'walking on eggshells'? A little research indicates that there is no consensus regarding where this idiom initially came from, however it is consistent with other such cautionary phrases such as 'walking on thin ice'. Generally, it is taken to mean taking appropriate action to avoid conflict with a particularly sensitive or reactionary person, where the difficulty of not upsetting said person in any way is comparable with the extreme challenge of walking on eggshells and not causing them to break – virtually impossible.

When Diana shared her story with me, I was fascinated to hear a slightly different take on this subject. Diana described the last years of her marriage as walking on eggshells around her husband. She did anything she could to avoid any kind of conflict, which often meant she resorted to being in a completely different room from her husband, thus avoiding him altogether. Essentially, she physically moved herself away so there was no danger of any noise associated with her presence that might alert him to the fact that she was around. She withdrew contact and effectively hid herself away.

The unusual factor associated with this story is that the fear expressed as walking on eggshells in this instance was not actually associated with the breaking of the eggshells but the noise that this breaking would create. She explained that she knew the relationship was already broken. Any noise therefore would have brought this situation out into the open and it would have to be dealt with.

Diana's retreat into silence clearly indicates the development of a coping strategy that was not congruent with her true authentic self. Invisible Diana was a construct, a mask to hide behind. The creation of this persona was a way to avoid facing the reality that she needed, by avoiding the inevitable conflict with her husband that would come when she voiced her truth.

Without getting involved in all the detail, it is possible to understand this story in the context of the framework I have created to understand how we disguise our truth and find ourselves living inauthentically. Initially, by the nature of her withdrawal Diana was actively suppressing her own individuality as a result of her response to the real or perceived needs of her husband. How can you be yourself if you avoid any communication by hiding in another part of your home, and if by such action you clumsily maintain the illusion of status quo mainly for the benefit of another?

This action is also indicative that she had compromised her inner personal integrity by not facing up to and doing what she knew was the right thing to do and what she really wanted, which was to end the marriage. The silence she created took away the influence of her own voice, as any opportunity to open a discussion was actively avoided. Her own admission of fear expressed as walking on eggshells meant that a fear of what might happen influenced her behaviour to such a degree that all power in the relationship was ceded to her husband, leaving Diana negligible impact in the relationship.

In her imagination, particular scenarios played out. By avoiding contact, the major conflict (that would eventually happen anyway) was diverted, however the resulting situation became an ongoing repeating pattern. For many years this served as a mechanism to avoid facing the truth, leaving no space to change and create a new future by forming an illusion in which the core existence appeared little altered and even less acknowledged. Maintaining this illusion, even at a distance, meant that Diana was unable to claim the independence she craved. As long as she allowed her husband to control the situation by virtue of the perception she had of what he might do if she voiced her wish to leave, she had made her own life dependent on him and was unable to break free. Her intuition was telling her that it was time to call a halt to this life that was no longer an expression of who she was, but it was a long time before she listened and took action.

Fear plays us in many ways, and here a fear of what might happen resulted in years of paralysis and inaction. Finally, however, enough was enough and she found the energy to shift, to leave and begin living life on her terms in full colour. The story does not, however, end there. Fast-forward some 17 years and Diana remained troubled by this period of walking on eggshells. She realised that she did not really know what it meant but that somehow on some level this aspect of her life was continuing to have an impact on her present situation. She decided to conduct a little experiment because she realised that she did not know what walking on eggshells actually meant. So, she tried it out, first removing the actual egg from inside. What Diana discovered was:

- Walking on eggshells does not actually hurt like you think it is going to

- It is actually gooey and sticky rather than painful

- It does not make much noise

There's the thing – not really painful, no real noise and it doesn't really hurt, just requires a bit of cleaning up after the fact.

What then can we learn from this exercise? For me, there are some clear messages:

- What we fear may not be as significant or have as much impact as we think

- You will never know the reality of something unless you give it a go

- Perception-led behaviour derives from inventing your own reality

- Your version of reality is likely to be very different from what you imagine as the reality of another

The final part of this story, after the eggshells had been walked on and the fears that had been carried for so long were debunked as myths, was the final shape of the smashed shells. Diana looked down and saw two hearts had formed: one positioned to show the inside of the shell, the other clearly the outside. She knew that this was another message: however broken her heart seemed on the outside, it remained whole inside and nothing could destroy that part of her. This was where she was fully her true self, where love lives.

Stuck on the carousel of life

Most of my clients are women, so this next person does not fit the 'template' for my ideal client. For starters, he is not female, is not getting divorced, has not lost his job and as he has never had children, is not suffering from empty nest syndrome. I am including his story in order to demonstrate that our adult patterns are very clearly formed by the events of our childhood, and although the outcomes may manifest differently, gender bias does not appear to be a factor in the ability to present an authentic persona to the world. Men hide too and this particular client is hiding behind the alternate masks of 'Mr Angry' and 'Mr Joker'. He is in a number of ways as lost as many women I coach, with these masks serving to deflect from reality according to the particular situation he finds himself in.

He does not know who he really is or what he wants to do, specifically what he wants to do with the rest of his life. His history revolves around being a 'short man' and to some degree always having to prove himself because of that. There are unresolved anger issues from childhood which have flowed through his entire life. His father died, told him to take care of his mother almost with his dying breath and the upshot was he never really had any choice but to take over the family business, which almost 40 years later he is still running.

During one particular session we followed a process that went very deep and the tears began to flow and they really did flow. His first comment afterwards was, "Do you always make grown men cry?" He has since admitted that he never cries and this really felt like an outpouring and release of all the bottled-up emotions from virtually his entire life. From my perspective this was a huge turning point and I have noticed a number of key changes in how he is dealing differently with the challenges in his life.

We also established that work (the business he took over from his parents) is his life and actually he does it for fun, but on the flip side work is also a hiding place from reality. It is a way of escaping to avoid having to deal with priority issues. The hamster wheel of work has actually become a prison too. Over the years the carousel of life continues to turn; all that changes is that he keeps getting on a different horse hoping that it will take him somewhere different. The carousel however keeps turning, same circuit, different day. It is time to get off the carousel horse, break out of the work hamster wheel and evaluate what he actually wants to do, something other than what has been decreed by others as the right path to take.

With every step there have been massive shifts and the results are beginning to show in respect of business, home, health and relationships. As getting organised progresses, breathing space has been created and this is where new things can now be visualised – finally there is room for something else. He is now able to think about what he wants to do next and plan for the future. I know that we have reprogrammed some of those embedded patterns in the neural pathways.

"When you change the way you look at things, the things you look at change."

Wayne Dyer

Chapter 14

Introducing the Reboot Protocol

Reboot – "(of a computer) to switch off and then start again immediately… to start something again or do something again, in a way that is new and interesting."

Cambridge Dictionary

As I worked with more people and started to see their results – the changes in their lives and the difference in themselves – I understood that they really were starting over and taking charge of who they were. Life had once more become interesting for them. As a process specialist it didn't take me too long to work out that what worked was pretty consistent for everyone. It was essentially the same process that I was following every time and so the Reboot Protocol was established.

Essentially, this was how my clients were switching off their old lives or aspects of their lives that needed change and restarting again in a way that was more interesting or made more sense to them. They were able to take huge leaps forward, understand the intrinsic reality of who they really were and start living life on their terms not the terms of somebody else.

Some people may associate this with taking back your power; however, I believe it goes beyond power and there is much more to it. Fundamentally it is about waking up to who you really are and taking ownership of yourself in all of your unique and special glory. It is about claiming your own thoughts, desires, needs, understanding your capacity to embrace whatever that may mean and no longer being too afraid, ashamed, guilty or shy to show that to the world.

The Reboot Protocol is simply a framework to work logically through the steps required using a variety of different tools at each stage and according to the specific needs of each individual. Each person may require more or less work on each aspect according to their own particular situation. The outline is straightforward; the result comes in the application and the only truth is in the results. It is not a magic pill and instant results are unlikely (although you never know what may happen until you begin!). Work is required to create the transformation you are looking for – after all, how many years of your life did it take to get to this point? Just like with weight loss, commitment and effort are required to create sustainable change. Such changes are designed to impact your life on many levels including work, relationships, health, emotions, spirituality, finances, family and ultimately your soul.

At each stage of the Reboot, it is important to evaluate every aspect of your life (often known as 'The Wheel of Life') to ensure that nothing is missed and consequently remains hidden from you, or you choose not to acknowledge certain aspects that you need to change. In addition, going deeper to the core of what is going on in each aspect of your life will also be looked at in the context of the ten facets of visibility we considered earlier, to establish exactly how you show up in the different areas of your life and where you are on the scale in these areas (Imbalance, Image, Identity, Individuality, Integrity, Influence, Impact, Imagination, Independence, Intuition).

This is particularly significant when you realise that we are all adept at using masks to present a reality to the world. As we often move in different spheres according to which particular aspect of our life we are engaged in at any given moment, then we will adopt different masks to deal with those scenarios and the people we encounter within them.

The steps of the Reboot Protocol are as follows:

Review your Life – Where are you now?

Evaluate your Energy – How is where you are affecting your energy?

Baseline your Vision – What would you like instead?

Organise your Objectives – How will you know when you have arrived?

Optimise your Plan – Exactly what steps do you need to make the change?

Transform your Soul – Live the life you want on your terms.

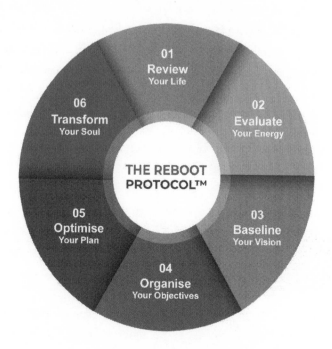

The Reboot Protocol Model

Nothing, however, can begin and nothing will change unless you first set your intention. This journey of transformation is designed to go deep, to address all areas of your life at the conscious and unconscious levels.

Intention

"Something that you want and plan to do…"

Cambridge Dictionary

"An intention is an idea that you plan (or intend) to carry out. If you mean something, it's an intention. Your goal, purpose, or aim is your intention. It's something you mean to do, whether you pull it off or not."

Vocabulary.com

Intention is the key to many things and their outcomes. Whatever happens to you in life can, for the most part, be linked to intention. If your intention is managed in the right way, that is with good and positive attachments that are rooted in love, then it is more likely that good things will happen to you and you will achieve the positive results you desire. Your words are also a clear indicator of your intention and not just the actual words you use, but the way you say them – your tone and emphasis for example.

If you are always using negative words in speech or thought, then you will most likely attract negativity. If you focus on talking about what you don't love, or what is wrong, then you will attract things you don't love – bad luck, poor health and so on. Likewise, in respect of your thoughts, the things you focus on – even the things you don't say – are picked up as your wishes, your requests to the universe, and you will manifest exactly what you ask for.

There is nothing new in this concept, it's all about the Law of Attraction and you will probably have heard about this from one source or another – perhaps you have watched or read *The Secret* or Napoleon Hill's *Think and Grow Rich*. Much has been documented already, however now I expect you, like me, are starting to realise that it may not be that simple to get what we want – or is it? For everyone who struggles with the concept, up pops someone else with the story of how they manifested a six-figure income and their dream home in what was apparently a matter of days. Let's get one thing straight: it is unlikely, unless perhaps they get a huge lottery win or similar. So, what really are your intentions all about and how does intention or lack of intention contribute to invisibility?

If intention is linked to having an aim or purpose, things that you plan and goals that you set, then an absence of all of those things won't actually lead to very much at all. If our thoughts are intentions and this is what the universe acts on, then clearly a lack of the right kind of intention in our thoughts – both conscious and just as importantly our subconscious thoughts – can lead to precisely what we don't want. If our thoughts focus on what we don't have then the most likely outcome is more of the same – more lack. Whether this is related to finances, love and relationships, employment, business, self-worth, any combination or all of these and possibly more is totally irrelevant if you are unable to be clear and consistent on what you really want.

Having less than honourable intentions also muddies the waters. If you set out to hurt someone or perhaps cheat in some way, for example financially or in a relationship, the likelihood is that the negativity and low vibrational energy attached to this behaviour and the intention that underpins it will in some way return back to you.

If you on the other hand are the injured party, your self-esteem may take a huge knock and your self-preservation instincts are likely to kick in so that you can protect yourself. In some situations, instinct takes over and becomes all there is. Your brain is fogged, your thinking unclear, and your ability to make decisions with clarity of purpose is simply overwhelmed and you may cease entirely to function on this level.

Ask yourself:

- Do I have an aim or purpose in life?

- Have I set goals for myself?

- Do I know what I mean to do?

- What chance have I got of achieving what I want?

- In general, are my thoughts mainly positive or negative?

- In general, are the things I say mainly positive or negative?

- Are my intentions towards others honourable?

- Where is my emotional vibration? Am I:

  ➢ Depressed

  ➢ Angry

  ➢ Blameful

  ➢ Frustrated

  ➢ Hopeful

  ➢ Enthusiastic

  ➢ Blissful

How does my emotional vibration affect my ability to act?

Most people have an unconscious ability to sabotage their supposed best intentions, because they are not aligned with a positive emotional vibration. Unfortunately, I see too many people who claim they want to change and yet their demeanour and the words they use indicate they are still firmly stuck in their own pity party, in victim mode. When we suffer through the trials that life throws at us, we come to understand that it is through facing and overcoming these we get results.

When you learn to set and stand by your boundaries be clear on your intentions, and 'fight your corner' in spite of what everyone else is telling you; only then will the right things that were always meant for you begin to appear in your life. When this shift happens, there needs to be no anger or malicious intent towards those who have wronged you, but instead a calm assertiveness and the clear knowledge that you must stand by what is right for you rather than acquiesce to the demands and shortcomings of others for the sake of an 'easy life'. You need to be clear and you need to understand your intention.

After all, when you think about it, is it actually so easy to give up the path or the things that you truly desire for yourself just to keep others happy and for the sake of the 'status quo'? When you start to look very honestly at where you have been denying your true feelings, your true self, in order to keep the peace, it is then a logical next step to move forward and claim what is yours. You have the right to be happy with yourself and your life. Now is not the time to be afraid of the consequences of doing this. Everything that is not meant to be in your life any longer, including people, will now start to disappear once you have moved forward into this next phase.

This natural clearing out makes way for all the things that are better for you, your sanity and self-care. Whatever and whomever are meant to stay and remain in your life will stay. That natural flow of life with all its ups and downs sometimes necessitates a letting go of relationships, situations and circumstances in order to make way for greater wealth on all levels. To clarify, we are talking about wealth of all kinds, not merely monetary. An abundant 'wealthy' life should really give a sense of balance. Whatever aspect of your life you examine should at the very least enable you to feel fully aligned with it. That it is meaningful, important and real for you and that it is really you.

If you have set your intentions, then let's dive right in and work out how we can switch off what you don't want in your life and get you started again in a way that is more aligned and truer for you. You may be wondering why Reboot, and what does this mean anyway? I'm sure you will be familiar with the concept of rebooting a computer, where the working computer is restarted using an aspect of hardware instead of the internal software. For example, switching off the power button. This may be necessary after new software or system updates have been installed and the device or the device drivers need to be re-initialised or restarted to fix an error.

As humans, from the day we are born we are constantly receiving system updates from the people around us and the surroundings and situations we find ourselves exposed to. Sometimes when things happen to us, we fail to 'compute' those changes effectively. We are unable to function as we are supposed to. We get brain fog, fatigue, headaches, aches and pains, illness and more. All of these can be linked to the emotional state we are in as a result of the specific inputs we have been receiving and attempting to deal with. Over time we are used to dealing with all of this information and process it effectively. In doing so we create the neural pathways that confirm our reality (Dr Joe Dispenza, for one, writes in detail about this topic). This information is then hardwired into our brains and becomes our reality. The way in which we make sense of the world, our truth, our perspective.

However, just like computers, sometimes things go wrong for us and we stop working properly. For example: our imagination may be fixated on one thing only, reliving something over and over again, perhaps trying desperately to make it better; we may find ourselves talking but people don't seem to hear us; our intuition seems to be broken because we make decisions that, even at the time of making them, we know they are not right for us. Our current reality may be so full of the noise caused by the situations and people we are involved with that we become too stressed out to identify what's important and what our priorities should be.

When dealing with a crisis, even if we are outwardly calm, we may well be on autopilot on the surface yet falling apart beneath – literally breaking. It's not my intention to discuss the labels that are sometimes attached to people in these scenarios when things bubble up to the surface and become apparent – emotional, depressed, crazy, schizo etc come to mind. There are many more, hopefully you understand where I'm coming from.

When a computer needs a reboot there's often too much going on at once and it simply doesn't have the processing or memory capacity to deal with it. Random Access Memory (RAM), the main type of memory in a computer, deals with all the short-term data and associated tasks. When you reboot, what happens is that all the random, temporary and largely unimportant data that is slowing down or crashing the device is literally flushed out. These days, computer operating systems can deal with minor problems as they occur, usually presented as a screen freeze or the circling icon that looks like it is the only thing working. In fact, it is working. What this signifies is the computer reaching a state from which it does not immediately know how to recover, hence why it stops the operation you want while it gathers information about the problem and then automatically restarts when it has sorted out the answer.

It can't just fix the problem without a reboot because when the code comes across a big enough problem, that problem completely stops it working and it simply cannot proceed. A reboot will start again from the beginning and if all is well the computer will not come across the same issue again. Unfortunately, many of us know from experience that sometimes problems get a little too big for a simple reboot and more work is required to provide a complete fix.

Q: What's clogging up your RAM right now that is stopping you from working properly?

Are you running slow, so that normal activities seem to take much longer than usual? You might not need to dredge through all the history and functional processes to find the exact source of the problem. If your capacity is simply being drained a simple reboot could fix the problem.

Perhaps specific programmes are being constantly re-run in your mind and just using too much memory, consuming so much that nothing else is able to work. Rebooting to deal with this issue can result in starting from a clean slate. With a computer the memory would be wiped; with people the memory remains but the result is a clean emotional slate, so the memory does not have the hold that it previously did. All the negative emotions – for example, fear, shame, anger and guilt – are removed from the memory so it no longer impacts the present.

What if it's a connection or network problem? Technologically speaking the software on your router may have come across a problem. A reset can be achieved by unplugging it and then plugging it back in. Likewise, if you have a communication issue – if you perceive that people are not listening or taking any notice of you – unplugging from that situation, or those people, and then rebooting so you are back to your high energy settings aligned with the real you could be a perfect solution. Walk away, so they'll miss you while you are gone and recognise that when you return. If of course you do return; that path may no longer be the one you are on and, if not, no matter, because the people you encounter from now on will see the truth of you – your light shining through.

In all scenarios, a reset wipes away the current state of the computer software. Any code that has got stuck or caused problems will have been removed. When you reboot, the computer will bring the system up from the beginning, restarting all the software so it will work just as well as it was before things started to go wrong. This is exactly what the Reboot Protocol is designed to achieve for you and your life.

"Our wretched species is so made that those who walk on the well-trodden path always throw stones at those who are showing a new road."

Voltaire

Chapter 15

The Ten Step Reality Check

Now it's time to dig a little deeper – take the Ten Step Reality Check and see if that makes a difference to how you understand your life today. I'm always asking "What's critical to resolve right now?" Different days may seem to highlight different issues, different priorities. At each stage we look a little closer, go a little deeper, think of it like peeling off the layers of an onion one by one and then examining what you see. The outer layers may be brown (or red perhaps) and crispy, there may be a little damage and bruising, perhaps a little yellowing to the flesh. Maybe the next layer is not as firm as you want so you still don't want to use it because it's a little squidgy and perhaps it's not as fresh as you need. So you go on until you get to a layer where the onion looks good enough to use. Then you slice, only to discover further damage below the layer you were just looking at. Luckily, it's only on one side so you can use the rest.

Sometimes though you peel through the layers and there's so much damage you can't use it because it would make your recipe taste horrible. Hopefully there is some to be salvaged to use and create something new and delicious. If it is good enough you will remember the taste of that dish – it will nourish you now and stay with you and you will know how to make it again. Just as every onion is not bad to the core, as we peel back our own layers we can discard the bad but find what remains good underneath. We can work with that.

Answer these ten questions to find out your Ten Step Reality Check Score. Read each question and give it a score from 0 to 10, 0 meaning that you don't agree at all and 10 meaning that you completely agree.

Ten Step Reality Check

1. Everything in my world feels just right and I feel content, with space to breathe.

0	1	2	3	4	5	6	7	8	9	10

Don't Agree   Completely Agree

2. I feel calm and in control of my life. My public image and my private self are aligned and I don't need to pretend or put on a brave face.

0	1	2	3	4	5	6	7	8	9	10

Don't Agree   Completely Agree

3. I know exactly who I am and where I am going. My life has direction and purpose.

0	1	2	3	4	5	6	7	8	9	10

Don't Agree   Completely Agree

4. I stand up for myself and what's right for my life even if this goes against other people's expectations and demands of me.

0	1	2	3	4	5	6	7	8	9	10

Don't Agree   Completely Agree

5. I do things that I want to do, because I put myself first and am able to say no to others when they ask too much.

0	1	2	3	4	5	6	7	8	9	10

Don't Agree   Completely Agree

6. I feel like the important people in my life listen to me and my opinions are valued and respected.

0	1	2	3	4	5	6	7	8	9	10

Don't Agree   Completely Agree

7. I feel fully alive with high energy to give to all aspects of my life.

0	1	2	3	4	5	6	7	8	9	10

Don't Agree   Completely Agree

8. My thought processes are clear and calm. I can easily make sense of my life and where I am going.

0	1	2	3	4	5	6	7	8	9	10

Don't Agree   Completely Agree

9. I feel supported with great friends and I'm able to move forward and enjoy life.

0	1	2	3	4	5	6	7	8	9	10

Don't Agree   Completely Agree

10. I trust myself and my judgment and have the confidence in myself to act in my best interests, in alignment with who I am.

0	1	2	3	4	5	6	7	8	9	10

Don't Agree   Completely Agree

Evaluate your results

If your score on the Ten Step Reality Check is **between 90 and 100,** this means you're in the **Green Zone**. Well done! You're doing great, keep it up! If you are not quite at 100, what minor changes could you make so life is even better?

If your score was between 70 and 89, this means that you are in the **Amber Zone**. You are doing OK, but be very careful you don't slip into the Red Zone. Work on what needs to be improved and aim to be even happier.

If your score was between 0 and 69, this mean that you are in the **Red Zone**. You are in danger of long-term problems if you don't do something about it. If you get working immediately with consistent commitment you can turn things around.

The Ten Step Reality Check was designed simply as a starting point to evaluate how things are right now. Bear in mind we are all dealing with many different things at any given moment in time and our current mood will certainly have an influence on how we answer. Tomorrow it may all look very different. There are very few people that can honestly say they are a 10/10 – that's ten out of ten in all aspects of their life all of the time. If you are in the Green Zone that's amazing, and let's hope you stay there!

There are, however, a few things to look out for. If you fluctuate between zones, green to red or green to amber, amber to red and so on, then you may well want to take a look at what's causing that. This is what systematically working through the Reboot Protocol will uncover as we look at every aspect at each stage, systematically moving closer to the truth of who you want to be and working on how you can get there. Life may not be entirely comfortable in some or even many respects; however, if your default position is not doing anything about it, by definition that becomes your comfort zone. Transformational change requires moving out of your comfort zone to the place where you can allow the magic to happen.

I'm sure you are familiar with this image, but I'll put it here anyway just to highlight the point.

Where the Magic Happens

One thing I have realised is that the times when I am furthest outside my comfort zone, my element, that's when I am closest to knowing who I really am and where I am more tuned in, so I actually experience myself more. If you are not in a familiar place, then things naturally feel different, perhaps you notice, sense, smell, feel, hear different things that you are not normally aware of. Things that have an effect of some kind on some aspect of your mind or body. It's discordant perhaps, feels uncomfortable, but you become aware of a different possibility.

When I see shooting stars, it's a magical awesome sight that stops me in my tracks, probably because I've not seen very many, but do you know how they are caused? When dust or particles from comets or asteroids hit the earth's atmosphere, they do so at high speed. Friction is caused as the dust comes in contact with air particles and heats them up. The heat then vaporises the meteors and creates the shooting stars that whizz across our sky.

When we venture down a path of change, emerging from our comfort zone, we take steps into the unknown and we encounter our own version of fresh air. Suddenly we can breathe differently, see things differently, and sure, there's friction because we are not used to this different air. We also have our subconscious doing its best to keep us safe in what we know. The battle between the unknown and the known can go either way, but when we persist, it's possible to create our own magic, be our own shooting star. Each step forward into the discovery of what's true is like unleashing a new bright star, until finally we light up so much we have created our own constellation that beams out our reality.

"Be who you are and say what you feel,
because those who mind don't matter,
and those who matter don't mind."

Bernard M Baruch

Chapter 16

The Reboot Protocol – Getting Started

I created the Reboot Protocol to work out what's wrong with the current state, locate the root causes of the problem, erase what no longer serves, sort out an appropriate fix or fixes and reset – maybe not to factory settings but to a point where you are able to start afresh feeling that everything is working as it was before things went wrong. Often things will work better, because much of the problem has built up over the years, its foundation based on events we no longer remember but reinforced by our learned responses to similar events we have encountered through life so far. Let's take a closer look at each of the areas.

Review your Life

As a process expert (I'm a Six Sigma Black Belt and have trained and coached hundreds if not thousands of people around the world to improve business processes), you soon realise that everything we do involves processes. One of my favourite examples is to ask a group of people to take two sticky notes and on one they write the first step they would take in making a cup of tea. On the second sticky note they write the last step – when they consider the process is complete. Although there may be similarities, invariably there are almost as many different first and last steps as there are people in the room.

The point of this in a business context is to illustrate that in order to improve a process everyone involved needs to be in agreement as to where the process starts and finishes. What are the parameters we are actually talking about and within which we need to find solutions?

With individuals, arguably the start of the process is when we are born, and the end is when we take our last breath. That's the high-level end to end process of life, yet it's essential to know which specific aspect we are looking at. If it's more than one aspect, it is important to identify the highest priority to work with first. There are processes to be uncovered in all areas of our life, work, home, family etc, and without getting too scientific or clinical it is possible to uncover the parameters within which we need to work.

There are a number of things that are vital to know before rushing off to fix things. If the preparation work is not done properly, the result is usually one of two things: either the wrong problem has been fixed, or the solution does not fix the problem. Whichever way you look at it you may possibly have fixed something; however, the issue you started with remains.

The first question I usually ask is therefore "What's the problem?" How easy is that to write or ask? The inarticulate and vague first responses, however, always demonstrate that while a business department, or a person in this case, knows that something is wrong, they can't quite put their finger on exactly what. That's when we look at all aspects of a process, in this case the process of life, to determine where the issues are and exactly how bad they are. Using my Ten Step Reality Check and an assessment of where a person is on the scale of each key pattern, we can start to build up a picture of what has gone wrong and the scale of the problem in each area. Understanding the problem is a vital factor in being able to move forward and this can sometimes be an extensive and emotional exploration.

Failure to review all aspects at this stage is like failing to do the proper preparation when you are redecorating a room. If the preparation is not done correctly the end result will not be great. When you simply paper over the cracks in a wall you will still be able to see the cracks under the new wallpaper. If you are anything like me that will then stay as an ongoing reminder of the damage underneath. The more you see it, the less it goes away.

With a business process, if you fail to understand the problem and the size of the problem at the start, that can result in solving the wrong problem and probably investing in and developing an ineffective solution that people think will solve the problem but actually doesn't. This is the reason why many IT solutions have failed to deliver what the users are expecting. It is a common human response to jump from problem to solution with a well-meaning, this will fix it intention. It is even more common to be horribly disappointed when it doesn't.

I'm not a fan of going over and over the 'old stuff' because that can prevent moving forward in any meaningful way. We need to explore enough, however, to ensure that we are not being continually reminded of the things we want to forget about the past when we have found a way forward. We need to make sure that we find out where all the cracks are, so we are not just papering over them and allowing them to stay in our present and future as opposed to making sure they are repaired enough to remain in the past.

Obviously, when we are talking about people, relationships, memories and so on we can't just erase them so they are completely forgotten. We can, however, take steps to make sure they do not control us in the new life we have created. This is why it is critical to understand energy as the next stage in creating transformational change – step two of the Reboot Protocol.

Your Action:

- Take a notepad, journal or sticky notes and considering all aspects of your life, write a list of all the things that you think are wrong with it, things that you are not entirely happy with.

- Next, sort your list into categories. This is where sticky notes work well as you can simply gather items from the same category together. Alternatively, you can just note (maybe colour-code or highlight) the categories next to each item on your list. Categories will include things like: health (H), finances (Fi), relationships (R), work (W), social life (S), family (Fa), friends (Fr), home environment (He), spirituality (Sp), learning (L). Feel free to add others relevant to your own particular circumstances.

- Now sort the categories into priority order. Rank them according to how important it is for you to resolve the issues in that category using a simple High, Medium or Low system.

- Finally, isolate the high priority list, and using a new journal page or sheet of paper for each, write one high priority item at the top of each page. Dealing with these issues will be where to focus initially.

Evaluate your Energy

Everything is energy. As Dr Joe Dispenza says, "Where your attention goes your energy flows." People who have heard me speak or who have attended workshops or groups that I have managed over the past few years, will know that understanding energy and working on the impact that energy has in our daily life has been a key theme in my research and presentations. There is far more to this topic than simply staying positive, downloading daily affirmations and chanting mantras. The platitudes of well-meaning friends and family such as, "Don't worry," "It will be all right," "Stay strong" and the rest are at times just as irritating as a mosquito on the loose in your bedroom in the middle of the night, and probably less effective at hitting their intended target.

I suspect, however, that most of us, often at a loss as to what meaningful words to say, have uttered such intentionally soothing phrases in our time. During the recent COVID-19 lockdown situations, with people around the world confined to their homes and communicating virtually, using computer and smartphone apps, I have encountered many 'rants' that people have posted on social media sites literally attacking people telling them to stay positive. "If one more person tells me to stay positive, it'll be over soon, we'll get through this…" You know the sort of thing.

Interesting how well-intentioned words are so badly received and produce anger rather than calm. Our energy is indeed volatile, and our responses to what is said to us or things that happen to us are constantly using and potentially draining our energy resources.

The way in which we respond, positive or negative, will require more or less energy resources and inevitably we will always get more of what we focus on. From the moment we are born, our brains, our memory, our neural pathways and connections are being programmed by everything that happens to us. In time our responses are learned responses because our unconscious knows exactly how this scenario plays out. Consciously we only ever deal with a very small part of what is actually going on inside our heads. The subconscious is actively processing and filtering billions and probably trillions of pieces of information every minute and as a result the response we make is based on what it knows or rather what we know. That knowing is based on our emotional responses, what our feelings were about something that previously happened to us. This is why you will always get more of what you focus on, whether that is positive or negative.

To give you an example, I used to have a journey to and from work that was 55 miles driving in each direction. It was always a horrible journey with accidents, roadworks, loads of traffic, and it was like that every single day, whatever time of day I made the journey. With hindsight, I worked out that after a few bad journeys I set the expectation that the trip was always going to be bad. I had experienced it, my mind was programmed to expect it, before I set off; my thoughts were always focused on how long it was going to take, how much traffic there would be. It is hardly a surprise then that the reality was exactly what I anticipated. I am still not entirely sure how it works but I do know that others using that same route did not have the same issues with the journey that I did. What was going on then?

Professor Brian Cox explains in his TV series *Wonders of Life* how "energy is always conserved, never created or destroyed" and that "every single joule of energy in the universe today was present at the Big Bang 13.7 billion years ago." When you put this into context, with the fact that everything in the universe is created from energy, is a manifestation of energy – that is humans, animals, trees and everything we see and hear around us — and that everything is therefore connected, the conclusion is that we create our own reality based on our own energy memories and also the energy of all that has gone before. Our thoughts create our reality.

I tested this theory on a long journey that had previously taken five hours to drive. I set the intention that the road ahead would be clear, with minimal traffic and no accidents, that traffic lights would be green all the way and without breaking the speed limit I could reach my destination in just under three hours. That is exactly what happened. I can tell you that five hours is pretty much an average for that particular trip at any time of the day or season of the year and three hours is more likely to be a fortunate one-off; however, I tested the theory a couple of times and it worked every time. It is now (when I remember) part of the planning process for pretty much any journey and it seems to hold true. Why not give it a go? I'll warn you though before you start that an important part of this is to truly believe that you can do what you believe you can. Feel the emotion of how you will feel when you reach your destination, safe and in good time.

The feeling of the emotion is a key factor in being able to create what you want. Basically, because you are bringing the emotion into the here and now, you are experiencing it here and now and therefore creating what it is you desire. If all your thoughts are focused on the bad things that have happened to you, the way someone made you feel for example when they did something that upset you, that is exactly where your energy will flow and that is why you will quite literally be drained.

Understanding exactly where your energy goes is a key step in being able to start making changes. We start this process during step two of the Reboot Protocol but it will also become embedded in the next steps and it will become a key area of focus to create real transformation. Inevitably when things slide a little, as they often do before becoming a natural part of our life, it's also the first area to look at.

- If you are always angry, the likely outcome is that more things will happen that make you even angrier. Look instead for things that make you calm and do more of those things.

- If you are sad and you can't seem to shift the sadness, finding something that makes you laugh, even for a moment, will create a little space in your energy field. Where there is a little space there is a chance for something new to enter.

- When you feel shame, ask yourself if you have really said or done something you regret or if this feeling stems from worrying about what other people might think.

If you do nothing else right now, be sure to watch your thoughts and the words you use. What do they tell you about the role you play in the world you currently find yourself in? Remember that energy will always take the path of least resistance. Don't make it easy to choose the wrong direction, because the further you head down the road you don't really want, the harder it will be to turn around and come back.

Your Action:

- Using the high priority items that you created earlier, consider your energy around each of the areas in turn. Make a note on the relevant page documenting the strongest emotion that you feel in relation to each of them.

- For the next week monitor your thoughts and the words you use around these high priority areas. For example, what sorts of things are you thinking and saying in your work situation? Note your findings and any insights on the appropriate page.

- Also, monitor where your information is coming from. What you hear from others, from the media etc, what you are reading or watching. All of this information will be landing in your subconscious and re-enforcing any old and negative patterns already there. Make a note of these and any insights that may follow.

Baseline your Vision

I have been creating vision boards for over 30 years now, since sometime in the late 1980s. At that time, we called them prosperity maps and actually I still quite like that concept. It adds a little more perspective to what we are talking about, and after all isn't that what we all really want? The buzzword these days is abundance and yet somehow that already feels a little tainted, outdated perhaps, possibly due to the industry that has emerged focused on exactly and entirely this topic. You don't have to look too far before another abundance-spouting 'guru' pops up in your life, or more likely your inbox. There is, however, much more to creating a vision than many so-called experts would have us believe.

As a business analyst frequently working with business owner clients at a strategic level one of the first things to establish is always what is the *Vision* of the organisation? From the vision flows the mission, the company objectives, then the strategy to achieve those objectives and finally the lower-level tactics – all the little things you do every day to make it work, that when successful have the cumulative effect of achieving the desired results. It is a process that is founded on the principle that if you don't know where you are going, how will you know when you have arrived there?

The same applies to any individual that wants to change their life. You have to shift from thinking about the past, through understanding why it has happened, how much it is impacting you in the present and look forward to what you want in the future. What do you want your future to look like? Who will be there with you? Where will you be living? How do you feel when you imagine yourself there? Imagine and really get in touch with those feelings and the emotions that bubble up to the surface. Think about every aspect of your life, your work, relationships, health, spirituality and so on. If you have a big issue with your health for example, you have to see yourself fit and well and living a full life (that is of course if that is what you really want). Remember to believe it and tap into the emotions that brings up.

If you are reading this and instantly doubting whether that is possible, just check out Brandon Bays' story of how she healed herself from a massive 'incurable' tumour. Read how Dr Joe Dispenza mended himself and walked again after doctors said there was nothing they could do for him. There are many more similar stories out there of people who take charge of their health by taking charge of their minds and their bodies. We still have a long way to go before enough people realise the power is within them and has been all along.

Knowing what you want in the future and all of the aspects associated with that is just a small part, the beginning if you like of creating your vision. Creating a vision board is also much more than cutting out pretty pictures, gluing them to a board and hoping that the things you want will magically appear. Ask anybody who says that vision boards do not work and that's probably exactly how they went about it. The same goes for the Law of Attraction, Manifesting Abundance, The Secret, and all the other similar strategies that are out there; they are not magic talismans and they will only work if you do, and of course if you know precisely where to look and how to unlock the magic that really is there.

Finally knowing where to look is the reason that I have now been able to purchase my beautiful house in Italy. For a long time it was an impossible dream and out of reach, but when I flipped the switch and truly believed that this specific house was mine, miraculously the process speeded up and so here I am. Before that point, it was sold at least twice. Naturally I was devastated but I held fast to my belief that this was my house and those sales fell through for a variety of different reasons – none of them to do with any problem or issue with the house itself. Now the house is revealing its energy to me and my soul is expanding beyond description into this space.

Of course, the picture of this very house was on my vision board for 2020, but believe me it took more than that to actually make it happen. These techniques I share in more detail in my workshops and with my coaching clients, but the truth is that if you really know what you want, if you believe that it is possible, if you can feel the emotion of achieving your vision and you refuse to give up, if you act as if it has happened, then you build up more and more space in your energy field and that is where you have the possibility to create new things. Once you have your vision then it's time to get to work.

Your Action:

- Think about what you want for yourself in the future. Take another sheet of paper or sticky notes and write down everything you want to see or have in your future. Be careful not to censor yourself. Don't let existing beliefs or knowledge or thoughts about what might be possible hold you back. Just go for it.

- As before, categorise what you have written into the relevant areas of your life that they apply to.

- Now return to the pages where you wrote down your highest priorities and note the relevant future aspirations underneath.

- Create a vision board – don't forget to put yourself in the centre of it!

Organise your Objectives

A vision is always the blue-sky big picture stuff, and of course there are a number of layers below. These are the goals, the objectives, the things you measure that tell you that you have achieved what you set out to. Every successful project will have a clear scope of exactly what you need in order to achieve the results that you are aiming for. Your objectives should also be measurable, for example within a specific timeframe – by when? a certain amount of money – how much? and also how well or how far the objective fits the initial requirement or vision. Remember, most people do not arrive at the place where change is necessary overnight (consider weight loss, addictions and so on in this context); however, many people still expect that a couple of coaching sessions will provide an instant fix for their issues.

Initially you may get some instant shifts that open you up to the possibility of there being something different – a different way, a means to move forward etc. The understanding of what has happened, the proverbial 'lightbulb moment', are each part of the foundation for creating change. Once you know where you are, how you got there and believe that things can change, it's time to get to work and determine the goals you need to achieve. The sum of these goals as a minimum will be the proof that you have achieved or are on the way to achieving your vision. Don't forget that you have to hold fast to your vision and there may well be incremental stages that will take you there one baby step at a time. It is impossible to climb a mountain in just one step.

I really do understand that, having stood at the top of Africa on the summit of Kilimanjaro, and gasped both in awe and for breath pretty much every step of the extreme trek to Everest Base Camp. Sometimes we need to remember to look around us during the trip. Whilst the destination may be the goal, there is so much to see and so many opportunities for learning along the way. Closer to home (in the UK anyway), Mt Snowdon is no walk in the park and the other 14 peaks known collectively as the Welsh 3000s each present their individual challenges.

Not every objective will be as tough as climbing a mountain; not everyone has either the desire or need to climb a mountain. It is useful to understand that we are all unique and have different challenges. One person's mountain will be someone else's hill. For some, that hill has all the proportions, risk and fear of the unknown that make it appear as big an obstacle as the highest of mountains. For everyone, grasping what is totally real and authentic to them and the size of their own personal mountain, that's what's important and that's how and why objective setting in this context is such a personal experience.

Whatever your personal objectives are, large or small, for next week, next year or far into the future, identifying them and understanding them is essential or you will never be able to say with any certainty that you have achieved what you set out to do. You also have to be specific so that you can monitor and measure as you go, understanding the progress you are making towards them. Even in a business context the things people want to achieve are often very vague. We find it very difficult to articulate exactly what we want. This is hardly surprising given that the very direct approach that we start with as children is for the most part conditioned out of us. I want an ice cream and I want it now is a typical approach for a small child. They know how to be very persistent and often will not give in. Tantrums may ensue if they don't get what they want.

I am not suggesting that you resort to having a tantrum to get your own way, but it is important to be able to articulate your desires clearly. It is also vital to remain consistent and stand firm in the face of challenge or opposition, which may well come in the form of well-intentioned advice from those closest to you. They want to keep you safe after all and they often think they know what's best for you. If what you want is legal, unlikely to intentionally hurt anyone and you believe it is what you really want, then ask yourself if it's about time you put yourself first. Look towards achieving your goals rather than helping everyone else with theirs first. Now is your time.

Your Action:

- Looking at each of the highest priorities you wrote down and the aspirations you recorded beneath them, write them down as more specific goals that you want to reach.

- Next, think about the activities, little steps you might take towards achieving each goal. If you make the steps too big, it may all seem too much and become overwhelming. If it's still too much to think about, pick the one that is your highest priority, the most critical right now and just work on that to start with.

- When you have done that, ask yourself how will you know when you have got there? It is important to make your goals and objectives measurable; for example, set a date (by when), a financial target (how much) and so on.

Optimise your Plan

Once you are clear on your vision and your objectives, it will be time to make a plan. I am so resistant to highlighting the frequently quoted 'when you fail to plan you are planning to fail', however it really does hold true for so much and so many, and for business and individuals alike. It doesn't really matter if Benjamin Franklin or somebody else said it first. Like many things in history, when you look deep enough it is possible to find a number of like minds all focused on developing the same concept. Consider manned flying machines for example; most people know that the brothers Orville and Wilbur Wright made the first successful manned flight but who remembers or has even heard of their greatest competition Samuel Pierpont-Langley? They each had their own plans focused on different aspects that they thought would achieve the results they were looking for.

Your task is to simply focus on your own plan without worrying about what anyone else thinks or what anyone else is doing. This is what you actually need to do in order to achieve your objectives and turn your vision into a reality. I see many competent professional people that are used to planning in a business context but have no idea where to start when it comes to their own life. It is almost as if all their energy is used up at work delivering results for the benefit of others so there is no space left over for them. How many people do you know whose work is their life and they have no room for anything else? That's usually when their home, relationships, health and the rest start to suffer.

So, we will create a bespoke plan that makes sense to you. Don't worry, I'm not going to make you use Microsoft Project (other project planning tools are available) or similar, unless that's what you really want and it fits with who you are and how you organise things so that they work for you. There are lots of ways in which we can do this, and it will evolve over time according to where you are on your particular journey.

To start with, many people, especially those in crisis, can only deal with detail actions at a weekly or in some cases a daily level. Some people can only commit to a couple of steps in between calls and that is absolutely fine. When you have a plan, any kind of a plan that you have developed, then you are more likely to take ownership of it and have a commitment to it. The obvious outcome is that you are more likely to get results. As I said at the start of this book, you already know most of this, and I know that if you think you haven't come across it before, in reality you will have in a previous incarnation. After all, this too is energy and it has always been with us and cannot be destroyed.

There are many ways to develop a good plan, but the secret to creating a great plan is to harness the power of limitless potential. Most plans are created from the historical past that we already know and cannot change and the predictable future, which also when you think about it derives from the historical past. By its very nature, planning can only happen because we already know things. The Cambridge Dictionary defines plan as *"a set of decisions about how to do something in the future"*, but what if we were able to create plans for our future based on what we don't already know? Now you know that's possible, it's time to make a plan to get you there.

Your Action:

- Review all of the activities you have written down against your goals in your priority areas, because now it's time to make them happen and set in motion the changes you want to create in your life. Determine if you know exactly what you need to do in each case.

- When you know what you need to do, it's time to work out how to fit these actions into your daily life. Some may be more straightforward than others. A very simple formula, often used in project management, is to consider: What do you need to stop doing altogether? What do you need to change? and What should you continue to do? I would add another parameter here: What new things do you need to start doing that you haven't done previously? You can apply this line of questioning around each priority, the relevant goals and associated activities.

- Look at your timeframe and pick a starting point.

Transform your Soul

When you are truly able to create a future from a new space, from a place where you know nothing, and there are no patterns to trip you up or divert you somewhere else (if there are, are you able to totally ignore them?), you can be massively innovative and create real transformation.

Of course, what we are talking about is taking action and making improvements, but it doesn't stop when we feel the first flush of success, when life starts feeling a little better and we are a bit brighter and more positive in ourselves. Improvement is all about constant review. Much of the time, when we have taken action we pat ourselves on the back then sit on our heels feeling smug that the job is done and we have put into place whatever we set out to do, maybe we have even achieved a goal. Implementation is, however, only the start. If you leave things at this stage, like a small plant that gets no sunshine or water, it will sooner or later wither and die. Any growth will be stunted and changes probably stagnated, maybe even reversed.

So, identifying and taking action to move towards your goals is just the beginning of the transformation. At this stage, much is coming from a place that is entirely known to you. It is the logical, the structured and the usual and it is a great starting place from which to begin altering your mindset and make changes. If you really want transformation though, it's important to go beyond what you already know and step into the unknown, the void. This is the space of infinite potential and limitless possibility. The good news is that it is accessible to you if you choose to believe it's possible. When you do, the sky is the limit – or maybe not even the sky. You can go as far as you can dream, if only you can go beyond what is already in your mind and make space to create something new. Naturally this takes some practice and requires some of our attention, pretty much on a daily basis. There are many tools and techniques that will lead you there, but for now we are jumping ahead.

This book can only really give you an overview and a starting point for some of the practices I use with my clients. It is but a brief introduction to the Reboot Protocol and the stages it goes through. The exercises are just a sample of the many that are in the toolkit. They are designed to get you thinking about where you are and where you actually would like to be and help you to set off on that path to a new you and a new life on your terms.

Your Action:

- Identify daily practices that will help you get in touch with your inner self to enable you to take time out and find that void where you will be able to create a future from the unknown zone rather than relying on what you already know. Daily practices will be different for everyone. They could include walking, cycling, running, yoga, meditation, swimming, mindfulness, breathing, Tai Chi, Qui Gong, the list is endless.

- Start journalling – focus on the good things happening and not the bad.

- Watch your thoughts and words constantly.

- Select or write some affirmations that support your journey.

- Breathe – really breathe, this will take you to the space you need, emptying your mind and focusing only on the breath.

- Live as if you already have what you want, believe it, see it, feel it, harness the emotions you will feel when you have achieved what you want.

When you learn to tap into those emotions at will, not only visualising your new home, relationship, body etc, but by physically feeling the emotion in the here and now, it is the emotions that will raise your energy. It is the emotions of your future that will overwrite the stored neural pathways of the past and ultimately change your present in order to create that future.

In summary, the key points to remember are relatively simple and if you do nothing else, at least do this:

- First believe in yourself, decide that it is all about you

- Know that it is already inside of you

- You already have everything you need

- Set your intentions

- Focus on your thoughts

- Notice where your energy goes

- Raise your vibration to embrace the unknown

- Listen to your intuition, it really does know the way

Your future is yours to create.

Namaste. I honour the divine within you.

"When you are content to be simply yourself and don't compare or compete, everyone will respect you."

Lao Tzu Tao Te Ching

APPENDICES

Appendix 1

The Last Word

This song is constantly running through my head. The Matt Monro version from the film soundtrack remains my favourite. I know it's about lions or one lion in particular. Elsa was rescued, rehabilitated and returned to the wild to live as she was meant to. We too are born free. Your life is worth living. Don't hide. Follow your heart. Need I say more?

Born Free

Born free, as free as the wind blows
As free as the grass grows
Born free to follow your heart

Live free and beauty surrounds you
The world still astounds you
Each time you look at a star

Stay free, where no walls divide you
You're free as the roaring tide
So there's no need to hide

Born free, and life is worth living
But only worth living
'Cause you're born free

(Stay free, where no walls divide you)
You're free as the roaring tide
So there's no need to hide

Born free, and life is worth living
But only worth living
'Cause you're born free

Songwriters: Don Black, John Barry

Born Free lyrics © Sony/ATV Music Publishing LLC

Appendix 2

Visibility Playlist

Music to wake you up! These are just a few of the songs of my life that never fail to cheer me up and remind me who I am.

Born Free - Matt Monro

What's Up - 4 non blondes

Man in the Mirror - Michael Jackson

Born to Be Wild - Steppenwolfe

True Colors - Cyndi Lauper

Walk on the Wild Side - Lou Reed

Free Bird - Lynyrd Skynyrd

Heroes - David Bowie

Rebel Rebel - David Bowie

Let's Dance - David Bowie

Every Little Thing She Does Is Magic - The Police

This is Me - Keala Settle & *The Greatest Showman* - Justin Paul, Benj Pasek

A Million Dreams - *The Greatest Showman* - Benj Pasek, Justin Paul

Catch a Falling Star - Perry Como

Happy Talk from *South Pacific* - Rodgers and Hammerstein

If by any chance you are feeling a bit down for whatever reason, just search in your internet browser for 'I Love to Laugh' from the 1964 film *Mary Poppins* with Dick Van Dyke and Julie Andrews. It really is infectious and practically impossible not to join in and laugh yourself. Give it a go, you know you want to. There is nothing quite like laughter to raise your energy level and provide an endorphin hit all at the same time!

Appendix 3

References

Bernard M Baruch (19 August 1870 – 20 June 1965) American financier, stock investor, philanthropist, statesman and political consultant.

Brandon Bays (born 21 August 1953) American motivational author and speaker.

Alexander Graham Bell (3 March 1847 – 2 August 1922) Scottish inventor and engineer credited with inventing the first telephone and co-founding the American Telephone and Telegraph Company (AT&T) in 1885.

Raymond Blanc (born 19 November 1949) French chef and patron at Le Manoir aux Quat' Saisons, a hotel-restaurant with two Michelin stars.

Bono (born 10 May 1960) Paul David Hewson known by his stage name *Bono*, Irish singer, songwriter, philanthropist, activist, venture capitalist and businessman.

David Bowie (8 January 1947 – 10 January 2016) English singer-songwriter and actor.

Claude Bristol (1891 – 1951) US journalist and author.

Coco Chanel, Gabrielle Bonheur 'Coco' Chanel (19 August 1883 –10 January 1971) French fashion designer and businesswoman.

Professor Brian Cox (born 3 March 1968) English physicist, best known to the public as the presenter of science programmes, especially the *Wonders of...* series.

Thomas Crapper (28 September 1836 – 27 January 1910) English businessman and plumber who founded Thomas Crapper & Co in London, a sanitary equipment company.

Wayne Dyer (10 May 1940 – 29 August 2015) American self-help and spiritual author and motivational speaker.

Bob Dylan (born 24 May 1941) American singer-songwriter, author and visual artist.

Dr Joe Dispenza (born 24 March 1962) American author, researcher and chiropractor, specialising in neuroscience.

Thomas Edison (11 February 1847 – 18 October 1931) American inventor and businessman described as America's greatest inventor. His inventions, including the phonograph, the motion picture camera and the electric light bulb, have had a widespread impact on the modern world.

TS Eliot (26 September 1888 – 4 January 1965) American-born British poet, essayist, publisher, playwright, literary critic and editor.

Ralph Waldo Emerson (25 May 1803 – 27 April 1882) American essayist, lecturer, philosopher and poet.

William Golding (19 September 1911 – 19 June 1993) British novelist, playwright and poet. Best known for his novel *Lord of the Flies* (1954).

Robert Holden (born 1965) British psychologist, author and broadcaster, who works in the field of positive psychology and wellbeing. Founder of the Happiness Project.

Steve Jobs (24 February 1955 – 5 October 2011) American, chairman, chief executive officer (CEO) and co-founder of Apple Inc., the chairman and majority shareholder of Pixar, a pioneer of the personal computer of the 1970s and 1980s.

Freddie Laker (6 August 1922 – 9 February 2006) English airline entrepreneur, founder of Laker Airways and one of the first airline owners to adopt the low-cost no-frills airline business model.

Lao Tzu, also known as Lao Tzu or Laozi. The *Tao Te Ching* is a Chinese classic text *The Book of the Way*, traditionally credited to the 6th century BC sage Laozi.

Philip Larkin (9 August 1922 – 2 December 1985) English poet, novelist and librarian. Offered but declined the position of Poet Laureate in 1984, following the death of Sir John Betjeman.

John Legend (born 28 December 1978) American singer, songwriter, record producer, actor, film producer, theatre director and philanthropist.

Helen Mirren (born 26 July 1945) English actor, National Youth Theatre, Royal Shakespeare Company, film actress.

Marilyn Monroe, born Norma Jeane Mortenson (1 June 1926 – 4 August 1962) American actress, model and singer.

Matt Monro, born Terence Edward Parsons (1 December 1930 – 7 February 1985) English singer who became one of the most popular entertainers on the international music scene in the 1960s and 1970s.

Friedrich Nietzsche (5 October 1844 – 25 August 1900) German philosopher, cultural critic, composer and poet.

Jamie Oliver (born 27 May 1975) British chef, restaurateur and television personality.

Natalie Portman (born 9 June 1981) actress and filmmaker with dual Israeli and American citizenship.

Tamar Posner Currently, an experienced psychotherapist based in London.

Gordon Ramsay (born 8 November 1966) British chef, restaurateur, writer and television personality.

Tony Robbins (born 29 February 1960) American author, coach and motivational speaker.

Sadhguru, Jaggi Vasudev (born 3 September 1957) known publicly as **Sadhguru**, Indian yogi and author.

Paballo Seipei, Currently a South African social media manager, content creator, Booktuber and book reviewer.

Dr Seuss, Theodor Seuss 'Ted' Geisel (2 March 904 – 24 September 1991) American children's author, political cartoonist, illustrator, poet, animator, screenwriter and filmmaker. Known for his work writing and illustrating over 60 books under the pen name Dr Seuss.

Socrates (470 – 399BC) Greek philosopher.

Rick Stein (born 4 January 1947) English celebrity chef, restaurateur and television presenter.

Sting, Gordon Matthew Thomas Sumner (born 2 October 1951) English musician, singer, songwriter and actor, principal songwriter, lead singer and bassist for rock band The Police.

Brian Tracy (born 5 January 1944) Canadian-American motivational public speaker and self-development author.

L J Vanier, Currently a journalist, author and blogger.

Leonardo da Vinci (14/15 April 1452– 2 May 1519) Italian thinker and inventor, considered one of the greatest painters of all time. The Mona Lisa is the most famous of his works and the most famous portrait ever made.

Voltaire, François-Marie Arouet (21 November 1694 – 30 May 1778) known by his nom de plume, Voltaire was a French Enlightenment writer, historian and philosopher famous for his wit, criticism of Christianity and advocacy of freedom of speech.

Oscar Wilde (16 October 1854 – 30 November 1900) Irish poet and playwright.

Mark Zuckerberg (born 14 May 1984) American media magnate, internet entrepreneur and philanthropist, known for co-founding Facebook.

Appendix 4

Further Reading

Ideas are Free - Alan G Robinson & Dean M Schroeder

The Journey - Brandon Bays

Becoming Supernatural - Dr Joe Dispenza

The Magic of Believing - Claude M Bristol

"Be proud of who you are,
not ashamed of how someone
else sees you."

Unknown

About the Author

Elizabeth Carney is a transformational coach, natural healer, business mentor and adviser. She has been called a 'soul-fixer'. Elizabeth uses a holistic approach to create the unique changes required by each individual. Clients experience transformation – releasing the past, rebooting and rebuilding an authentic life on their terms.

A 25-year international corporate background alongside lifelong study of natural and energy healing modalities (Vibrational Sound Therapy, Reiki, Rahanni, Shamanic healing, and essential oils) places her in a unique position that spans the world of business processes and the processes of life and living.

An accredited Master Coach with a BA in Communication Studies and an MSc in Education and Training Management, Elizabeth also has a Diploma in Business Analysis and is a Six Sigma (Process Improvement) Black Belt.

In 2020 Elizabeth moved to Italy to restore a wonderful old house to its former glory. The house is majestically perched on a ridge in the midst of the local vineyards and olive groves with breathtaking mountain views and the Adriatic just around the corner.

She is currently coaching online and looks forward to welcoming more visitors, VIP Intensive coaching clients and small intimate retreats at the house.

Website: https://elizabethcarney.co.uk
Email: liz@elizabethcarney.co.uk

Taking ownership of the Pink House, Abruzzo, Italy
Watercolour by Patrick Kelly based on a photograph taken on
7 July 2020